"The inspiring practices backed by science in *The [Self-Compassion Daily Journal]* unlock a new level of acceptance, fulfillment, and performance. [Diana Hill's] variety of inspiring compassion as a skill is a must-have [toolbox] to navigate [life's]. [The] practices help create space to take the full breath you didn't know you needed. Her impactful writing and clarifying questions are inspiring, and make the experience unique and fun."

—Sonya Looney, MS, NBC-HWC, world-champion professional mountain biker, and host of *The Sonya Looney Show* podcast

"In *The Self-Compassion Daily Journal*, skilled psychologist and meditation teacher Diana Hill offers you a warm, wise, and effective real-world path through life's difficulties. You will learn to listen to and respond to yourself with kindness, identify what an enriching life means to you, and through these powerful practices gain the courage to extend your compassionate heart to others."

—Trudy Goodman, PhD, and **Jack Kornfield, PhD**, founders InsightLA and Spirit Rock Meditation Center

"Diana Hill is back with more support for growing a deep, satisfying, stress-defusing life. Her new workbook is a 'kind hand on our backs' as each of us navigates the unrelenting pressure of self-criticism. Activities include befriending ourselves, establishing a soothing breathing practice, unsticking our cycle of oppressive thoughts, and working with hopelessness using our creativity. Hill's work is grounded in reality and offers practical help, even while exploring the latest research-backed theories in the field of self-compassion."

—Julie Bogart, creator of the Brave Writer program, and author of *Raising Critical Thinkers* and *The Brave Learner*

"Diana Hill offers a rare combination of therapeutic insight and friendly support, grounded in both scientific research and contemplative wisdom. Wow. This is a gem of a book that will help anyone live with greater confidence, courage, and inner peace."

—Rick Hanson, PhD, author of *Resilient*

"How can we harness the power of self-compassion to work with our inner critic and nurture the courage, wisdom, and commitment we need to address suffering and cultivate a caring, aware, open, and purposeful life well lived? *The Self-Compassion Daily Journal* is an excellent, elegant, and powerful guide that helps readers do exactly that, inviting them to water the seeds of compassion and psychological flexibility daily."

—Marcela Matos, PhD, auxiliary researcher and professor at the University of Coimbra, Portugal

"Cultivating self-compassion requires practice, and that works best with a structure and a guide. Diana Hill has provided you just such a step-by-step approach to maintaining your self-compassion practice with *The Self-Compassion Daily Journal*. Beyond that, she is a wise and caring guide who can help you to go farther than you might expect in your journey into mindfulness and compassion. I'm recommending this book to my clients and students, and to you!"

> —**Dennis Tirch**, founding director of The Center for Compassion Focused Therapy, and author of *The Compassionate-Mind Guide to Overcoming Anxiety*

"Diana Hill is brilliant at making important ideas accessible to us all. In small, bite-size units, this gentle and wise book will help you create habits of compassion that will touch and lift up every corner of your life. Structured as an eight-week journey into what your heart yearns for, it never overwhelms, never talks down, and never lets you flounder. It takes you by the hand, treats you as an equal, and shows you how to master skills that matter. An awesome piece of work."

> —**Steven C. Hayes, PhD**, professor of psychology emeritus at the University of Nevada, Reno; and originator of acceptance and commitment therapy (ACT)

The
Self-Compassion
DAILY JOURNAL

Let Go of Your Inner Critic &
Embrace Who You Are with
Acceptance & Commitment Therapy

Diana Hill, PhD

New Harbinger Publications, Inc.

Publisher's Note

NEW HARBINGER PUBLICATIONS is a registered
trademark of New Harbinger Publications, Inc.

In consideration of evolving American English usage standards, and reflecting a commitment to equity for all genders, "they/them" is used in this book to denote singular persons.

Distributed in Canada by Raincoast Books

Copyright © 2024 by Diana Hill
New Harbinger Publications, Inc.
5720 Shattuck Avenue
Oakland, CA 94609
www.newharbinger.com

Cover and interior design by Amy Shoup

Acquired by Elizabeth Hollis Hansen

Edited by Joyce Wu

Library of Congress Cataloging-in-Publication Data on file

Printed in the United States of America

26   25   24

10   9   8   7   6   5   4   3   2   1   First Printing

For my parents, Helena and Gary,
my first teachers in compassion.

Contents

Foreword

In a world of relentless hurriedness, it's easy to fall into the trap of self-criticism, measuring our worth by our productivity and by other people's opinions. Many people have two responses to self-criticism. They push themselves harder to be good enough, releasing stress hormones into their body and making themselves sick, or they give up. Is there another way?

In our struggle to overcome self-criticism, we often overlook the transformative power of self-compassion—the practice of treating oneself with the same kindness, empathy, and understanding that we would offer to a close friend. Self-compassion involves nurturing our own well-being, acknowledging our faults without harsh judgement, understanding our own pain, and providing ourselves the support and care we need.

The Self-Compassion Daily Journal is a timely guide, a compass for those lost in the whirlwind of self-criticism and self-judgment. It invites you to embark on a healing journey, one that empowers you to let go of your harsh inner critic and make room for a supportive, nurturing voice. It asks for just a few minutes of your day, providing a simple and manageable way to integrate self-compassion into your daily routine.

Many people fear that if they show themselves compassion, they will be less successful and less effective, or they will become "lazy" or lose motivation. Rest assured, research does not support this idea. People who treat themselves with compassion and stay committed to their values during hard times are happier and more effective. In particular, people who practice self-compassion are more resilient (Marshall et al. 2015), better able to take negative feedback (Leary et al. 2007), have more motivation to improve after a mistake (Breines and Chen 2012), and higher reengagement with goals (Neely et al. 2009).

What's more, hundreds of scientific trials show that the methodology this book adopts, acceptance and commitment therapy (ACT), helps individuals live more enriched lives by promoting psychological flexibility and encouraging acceptance of experience. Through a combination of writing prompts, guided meditations, and practical exercises, this book guides you toward an unshakable acceptance of self and a renewed commitment to growth.

In reading this book, I encourage you to engage deeply, to be patient with yourself, to be open to change, and most importantly, to be kind to yourself. Remember, this is not a race or a competition; it's a journey toward self-understanding, self-acceptance, and, ultimately, self-compassion. By spending a little time each day, you'll be making steady progress without being overwhelmed.

As you read these pages, I hope the insights provide you with direction if you find yourself adrift in a sea of self-doubt or self-criticism. No matter how dark the storm of self-judgment gets, the compass needle always points toward acceptance, resilience, and unwavering faith in yourself.

May your journey be enriching and healing. May you find that every small investment in time brings you closer to the serenity and love you deserve.

—Joseph V. Ciarrochi, PhD

A Kind Hand on Your Back

Do you tend to be harsh with yourself when you're struggling? Do you wish your inner critic would stop giving you such a hard time? Do you want to be kinder to yourself?

You're not alone. We all want to feel encouraged and cared for, especially when we're hurting. And it's often easier to offer compassion to others than to ourselves. Self-compassion is a way of relating to yourself that helps you feel more grounded, less alone, and more cared for when facing uncertainty and pain. With self-compassion you can let go of your inner critic and develop a new voice, one that gives you the courage to face hard things and the commitment to make positive changes that benefit not only you but everyone around you.

We all could use a kind hand on our back.

The *Self-Compassion Daily Journal* is an eight-week collection of guided journal prompts that will help you make self-compassion a habit, one page at a time. You'll learn to place a kind hand on your own back and support yourself when you need it most.

To thrive during challenging times, it's important to learn to:

- Stay aware and centered
- Step back from judgmental thoughts
- Offer yourself warmth and encouragement
- Tune in to and care for your body
- Forgive yourself when you make mistakes

- Be courageous and take action toward what matters most
- Keep at it, moment to moment

Nobody is immune from suffering. We all do things we regret, face sudden bad news and feel the stress of life's uncertainty. At its foundation, self-compassion is extending the same help to yourself that you would to a good friend in distress. With awareness, understanding, and love, you can better tolerate emotional difficulties, grow from your mistakes, and make healthier decisions.

Let the *Self-Compassion Daily Journal* guide you to respond to yourself in challenging moments with warmth and wisdom, so you can move toward what you care about without inner pain stopping you.

Give yourself eight weeks to try it out, and you just might find that self-compassion gives you, as it has me and my clients, the support you need to meet your imperfections and life's challenges with a brave and kind heart.

What Brought You Here?

When clients start therapy with me, instead of beginning with their list of problems, I go for a deeper question: What is it that you care about that brought you here? Take a moment and ask this question yourself. If you're immediately inspired, you could jot some thoughts down now. But you don't have to have an answer or write anything down...yet. You can also let yourself linger on that question.

By the end of this journal, I hope that what you discover supports you in expressing that care in the world.

The aim of this journal is to nurture your greatest inner resource: a caring and courageous heart. Often what matters most to you is also what's most painful. With self-compassion you can grow the life you want, without your inner critic getting in the way.

Paul Gilbert, the creator of compassion focused therapy, describes compassion as having two parts (Gilbert and Choden 2014):

1. Engagement: turning toward pain and suffering

2. Alleviation: taking action to alleviate pain and suffering

By acknowledging your suffering and giving yourself what you really need, you can better tolerate hardship *and* better be there for others. Self-compassion isn't always easy and, at times, can mean making hard decisions that are better for you in the long run. Your compassionate self wants what's good for you, even though it's uncomfortable. With self-compassion, you can achieve what you hope to achieve in life *while* feeling nourished by your own kindness.

You may think that being self-critical motivates you to change, but research shows quite the opposite is true. Self-criticism lowers your self-confidence and increases anxiety and depression, undermining your ability to take steps toward change. Criticism can also become a habit that's aimed at other people in addition to ourselves. With self-compassion you can take the energy you put into beating yourself up and put it toward making positive changes. You're less likely to get stuck in cycles of shame, are better able to stick with hard things, and have more compassion for others.

What if the next time you were having a hard time you had someone at your side who was encouraging and wanted the best for you? How would that change your experience? What if that someone could be you?

Self-Compassion Takes Psychological Flexibility

The *Self-Compassion Daily Journal* integrates principles from compassion-based therapies (compassion focused therapy, Gilbert and Choden 2014; mindful self-compassion, Neff and Germer 2018) and acceptance and commitment therapy (ACT).

ACT is an evidence-based approach to human flourishing that teaches you strategies to grow your *psychological flexibility*. Psychological flexibility involves staying present, open, and engaged in your values, even in the face of obstacles (Hayes, Strosahl, and Wilson 2012).

The ACT core processes are woven throughout this journal:

- Being present
- Taking perspective
- Acceptance
- Cognitive defusion
- Valuing
- Committed action

If you want to learn more about ACT, you may want to complete *The ACT Daily Journal: How to Get Unstuck and Live Fully with Acceptance and Commitment Therapy.*

How to Use This Journal

Each week in the *Self-Compassion Daily Journal*, you'll discover a new aspect of self-compassion and apply it through daily writing, experiential exercises, and life practice.

The weeks build on each other, so that day by day, week by week, you deepen your understanding of what self-compassion means to you, *in your life.*

Like any skill, self-compassion takes practice to make it a habit. Be creative and flexible when practicing with this journal. For example:

- Play Russian roulette—turn to a random page and complete it
- Savor the journal and do one chapter a month
- Read through the journal first without writing anything
- Find a self-compassion buddy and meet weekly online or in person to exchange thoughts
- Share your writings with your therapist, coach, or mentor

The most important thing is that you're kind to yourself in the process. Enjoy a cup of tea, use your favorite pen, and savor the process of taking this time for yourself (even if it's only for a few minutes a day)!

As we begin this self-compassion practice together, I am imagining putting my hand on your back, wherever you are, and offering you encouragement and well wishes. I hope that you will imagine that too. By the end of this journal, I hope you can do that for yourself.

A Hopeful Path

Everyone is worthy of care, including you, but caring for yourself doesn't always come easily. This week you'll explore your hopes and fears about self-compassion.

Think back to yesterday—check if at any point you felt:

O Anxiety

O Boredom

O Irritability

O Low mood

O Cravings

O Physical pain

O Fatigue

You're not alone. It's likely that people around you were feeling similar things but not saying it. Culturally, we're trained to push away what doesn't feel good. You've probably heard well-meaning advice like:

- Cheer up

- Distract yourself

- Get over it

Although this advice isn't inherently bad, it can send the message that it's your job to fix bad feelings fast! When you can't, you might feel like there's something wrong with you.

Have you received the message that if uncomfortable feelings show up you should fix them?

Yes   No

Do you sometimes feel like there's something wrong with you when you're feeling bad?

Yes   No

Have you been told you're overreacting when you're upset?

Yes   No

In today's feel-better culture, we're often taught to control negative feelings. The wisdom traditions, and now modern psychology, offer something radically different: *True freedom comes when we can hold all experiences, including the hard ones, with compassion.*

To paraphrase ACT cofounder Steven Hayes, instead of trying to *feel better*, we need to *get better at feeling* (Hayes, Strosahl, and Wilson 1999).

In the days ahead, instead of turning away from difficult experiences, you'll learn to care for yourself while you're having them. Your current ways of relating to yourself may not be working for you, but that doesn't mean you're hopeless. There's hope in trying a different approach.

DAY 1: Hopes for Self-Compassion

You likely have some hopes for yourself in starting this journal, which is great. Hope can encourage you when your motivation to journal wanes—which it will. At some point, you'll likely ask yourself, *Wait, why did I want to do this journal thing in the first place?* Let's answer that question together up front.

Take a moment to reflect on what you care about that brought you here. What are you hoping to achieve with self-compassion practice? If you could meet yourself eight weeks from now, what would you like to see?

_____

_____

_____

_____

_____

_____

_____

Having hope involves having *agency* in your perceived ability to pursue your goals—"I can do this"—and *pathways* to generate possible routes to achieve your goals—"I can find a way to get this done" (Weis and Speridakos 2011). What personal strengths can you draw on to help you keep up your journaling practice? And how do you plan to do it?

_____

_____

_____

_____

_____

In what ways can you be flexible with yourself while also achieving the goal of daily-ish journal practice?

_____

_____

_____

_____

_____

_____

_____

_____

_____

_____

_____

_____

🌑 **TODAY'S PRACTICE.** Keep in mind the image of yourself eight weeks from now. Do one thing that embodies that version of you today.

DAY 2: Fears of Self-Compassion

Having compassion for yourself can have a powerful positive impact. But your beliefs about self-compassion may block you from actually doing it. You may think self-compassion is not going to work, or even fear it. Do you relate to any of these beliefs?

○ If I'm gentler with myself, I won't work as hard

○ If I feel my feelings, I'll be overwhelmed by them

○ If I'm self-compassionate, I'm being selfish

○ I don't deserve to forgive myself

○ Self-compassion is weak

○ If I'm not self-critical, my flaws will show

Fears of self-compassion can prevent you from caring for yourself when you need it most (Gilbert et al. 2011). When you believe that self-compassion leads to complacency, indulgence, or irresponsibility, you're less likely to practice it and, thus, less able to adaptively cope to emotional challenges (Chwyl, Chen, and Zaki 2021). For example, in a survey of over four thousand people in twenty-one different countries during COVID, people who feared compassion had increased anxiety and depression and decreased feelings of social safeness (Matos et al. 2021). Let's look at your beliefs about self-compassion head on.

Do you think self-compassion might have downsides? Do you have any fears about it? What are they?

_____

_____

_____

_____

Why do you think these beliefs and fears developed?

_____

_____

_____

What else blocks you from being caring toward yourself?

_____

_____

_____

What do you hope would happen if you could be more self-compassionate?

_____

_____

_____

_____

_____

_____

_____

_____

_____

_____

🌑 **TODAY'S PRACTICE.** Notice times when you could be kinder to yourself. What fears or beliefs block you from choosing self-compassion?

DAY 3: Befriending Yourself

Yesterday you explored some of your beliefs and fears about self-compassion. Today you're going to distinguish self-compassion from some common misconceptions about it. Remember that self-compassion is treating yourself the way you would a good friend. As you read the lists below, consider the qualities of a good friend.

Self-Compassion Is:	Self-Compassion Is Not:
Believing you have worth	Being self-absorbed
Genuine humility	Self-pitying
Asking yourself what you really need	Always getting what you want
Feeling connected	Feeling better than
Holding yourself accountable	Letting yourself off the hook
Being supportive and understanding	Being lazy
Being forgiving	Being right
Active	Passive

What are the qualities you look for in a good friend?

_____

_____

_____

_____

_____

Which of these qualities would you like to offer more to yourself?

_____

_____

_____

_____

_____

Looking at the day ahead, which quality do you need most to meet its challenges?

_____

_____

_____

_____

TODAY'S PRACTICE. Get out a sticky note and write down one quality of friendship you want to give yourself today. Put it somewhere you can see it.

DAY 4. Sidestepping Suffering

Self-compassion involves learning to acknowledge and understand your emotions and face your difficulties with openheartedness. This might go against how you usually relate to yourself. Our biology, learning, history, and culture often direct us to ignore uncomfortable sensations, fix bad feelings, and push negative thoughts away. Although this may bring relief in the short term, in the long term, thoughts and feelings can rebound stronger. And instead of building the life you want, you spend a lot of energy trying to not feel bad.

In ACT, when avoiding discomfort turns you away from your values, it's called *experiential avoidance*. In week 4, you'll gain skills to open up to accept your inner experience. Today let's look at how you're shutting it down.

Consider something that is challenging for you right now. What do you do to avoid your thoughts and feelings about it?

- O Try not to think about it
- O Distract yourself
- O Numb out with substances, food, or technology
- O Problem solve or overintellectualize it
- O Give up, avoid going, or isolate
- O Brace your body and tense up
- O Blame yourself or others

What else do you do to control or avoid difficult experiences?

_____

_____

_____

_____

_____

_____

When you do these things, how does it feel in the short term?

_____

_____

_____

How do you see experiential avoidance affecting you long term?

_____

_____

_____

_____

_____

_____

_____

_____

_____

_____

⬤ **Today's practice.** Pay attention to the ways you avoid discomfort. Ask yourself, _Is this helping me in the long term or making things worse?_

DAY 5: The Costs of Criticism

Another common block to self-compassion is our inner critic. We all have a voice (or many voices) inside our head that judges what we do and gives us negative feedback. Our inner critic may have evolved to help us avoid pain, protect us from making mistakes, or keep us part of the group. But in current times, the inner critic tends to do more harm than good.

When you believe that critical voice, it demotivates you and intensifies the very pain you're trying to avoid. What's worse, listening to your inner critic can prevent you from doing things you love and trigger unhealthy behaviors. Habitual self-criticism can also make us more likely to be critical of others.

In week 3, you will learn skills to defuse from your inner critic. First, let's take a realistic look at the consequences of believing it.

What is your inner critic particularly hard on you about? When is it loudest?

_____

_____

_____

_____

_____

_____

_____

What happens when you listen to your inner critic? What are the short- and long-term consequences for you?

_____

_____

_____

_____

_____

_____

_____

How does your inner critic affect your work, relationships, or health behaviors?

_____

_____

_____

_____

_____

How would life be different if you didn't give your inner critic so much power?

_____

_____

_____

_____

Today's practice. Notice your inner critic today. Ask yourself, *Is this voice helpful to me in reaching my goals?*

DAY 6: Creative Hopelessness

This week you've explored common blocks to self-compassion:

- Fears or beliefs about its downsides
- Experiential avoidance
- Self-criticism

You've also looked at the short- and long-term consequences of avoiding pain and being hard on yourself. It can be discouraging to focus on what is not working for you. On the other hand, this can open you up to new possibilities—what ACT calls "creative hopelessness." It's hopeless to keep criticizing yourself if it ultimately makes you feel worse, and hopeless to keep avoiding pain when doing so limits your ability to pursue your goals. But when you fully acknowledge these points, you have the opportunity to try something different.

Hopeless behaviors: Looking back on what you wrote this week, what do you notice are your biggest blocks to being kind to yourself?

_____

_____

_____

_____

_____

_____

_____

_____

_____

Creative behaviors: Where might self-compassion be most helpful to you? If you could face your anxiety, anger, and sadness with courage, what might you be able to do that you aren't doing now? If your self-critic weren't running the show, what risks would you take?

_____

_____

_____

_____

_____

_____

_____

Find fresh hope: Could you do anything differently this week? What would you like to continue to practice and expand on?

_____

_____

_____

_____

_____

_____

_____

● **Today's practice.** Notice moments when you feel stuck in old patterns of fear, avoidance, or self-criticism. Try something radically different.

DAY 7: Soothing Rhythm Breathing

Have you noticed that when you walk in the door after a stressful day you take a big sigh? (Feel free to take one now). Or that when you feel content, your breath slows down? Slow breathing, especially on the exhale, activates the parasympathetic branch of your nervous system via the vagus nerve, which downregulates your body's stress response (Porges 2022). Today you're going to learn a simple breathing exercise from compassion focused therapy (Tirch, Schoendorff, and Silberstein 2014) called soothing rhythm breathing.

Soothing rhythm breathing centers you, helping you feel safe and at home in the present moment.

Let's practice together. Download an audio file of this practice at http://www.newharbinger.com/53496. Rate yourself (0 = not at all to 5 = very) before and after your practice.

	Before breathing (0–5)	After breathing (0–5)
How present are you?		
How centered are you?		
How connected to your body do you feel?		
How much tension do you feel?		

Take long, slow breaths through your nose. Find a pace that's not forced and feels soothing. If you like, you can add mantras or short phrases like this one from Thich Nhat Hanh: "Breathing in, I am here; breathing out, I am home."

Complete at least five cycles.

What happened when you practiced breathing in this way? When do you think soothing rhythm breathing would be most helpful to practice?

_____

_____

_____

_____

_____

_____

_____

_____

_____

_____

_____

_____

_____

_____

_____

_____

● **Today's practice.** Choose a time to practice soothing rhythm breathing for a few minutes. Link it to another activity you do daily, so that you will repeat it again tomorrow (like journaling!).

Reflection

This week you *explored your hopes and fears about self-compassion.* You also looked at some of the *costs of avoiding discomfort and being self-critical* and explored how to use *creative hopelessness* to motivate you to try something different. Finally, you learned the core self-compassion practice of *soothing rhythm breathing.* Think back over the exercises you tried. Which ones were the most helpful for you and why?

_____

_____

_____

_____

_____

_____

_____

_____

_____

_____

_____

_____

_____

_____

_____

_____

A Compassionate Perspective

One day as I led a new client down the hall, she said, "You may want to fix your skirt." It was fully tucked into my underpants. I was mortified! Thankfully, she said, "Don't worry, we all get our skirts stuck in our underpants sometimes."

It's normal to feel anxious, embarrassed, or even mortified sometimes. Seeing your mistakes and imperfections from a compassionate perspective makes being human more bearable—at times even humorous.

Perspective taking is a core process of psychological flexibility that helps you observe your experience and see it in context. When you take a *self-compassionate* perspective, you view yourself through the eyes of someone who is wise, encouraging, and who wants the best for you.

Consider a problem you're having right now:

If someone you loved had the same problem, how would you help them?

_____

_____

_____

_____

_____

_____

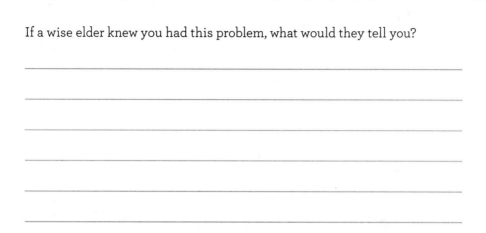

If a wise elder knew you had this problem, what would they tell you?

_____

_____

_____

_____

_____

Three Components of Self-Compassion

A compassionate perspective has three qualities: mindfulness, kindness, and common humanity (Neff 2021).

Mindfulness allows you to observe and stay with whatever you're feeling, rather than running away, compulsively fixing, or distracting yourself. You can simply ask yourself, *What am I feeling in this moment?*

Kindness is holding yourself with understanding and warmth. It's checking in to ask, *How am I doing right now?* Then validating your emotions (*It's understandable I feel this way*) and offering help (*I'm here for you*).

Finally, your *common humanity* with others means we all face hardship—and if you're feeling something, it's likely someone else has felt that way too. Acknowledging that we're all united in our experiences of pain and joy helps you feel less alone.

DAY 1: Be Here Now

It's hard to care for your feelings if your mind is so distracted, you're not present for them. And it's hard to give yourself what you need if you don't notice you have needs! Fortunately, you can train your mind to stay aware and checked in throughout your day.

For example, my family has mindfulness bells ringing on our devices—including the kids'—every hour. Often when the bell rings, I'm caught up in thinking about the future, rushing from one thing to the next, or multitasking. The bell gently brings me back to life here and now. You can choose an alarm, a mindfulness bell app, or another cue to trigger your mindful attention practice. Here are some examples:

- Take the first sip of tea or coffee mindfully
- Take three breaths before starting your car
- Look your loved one in the eyes when you greet them
- Don't pull out your phone when standing in line
- Before going on social media, do a mindful check-in

Where do you want to be more present in your life? How would being more present in your life benefit you and those around you?

_____

_____

_____

_____

_____

_____

Pause and get present with three slow, soothing rhythm breaths. What do you notice in the here and now?

_____

_____

_____

_____

_____

_____

_____

● **Today's practice.** Choose a cue to remind yourself to bring your attention to the present moment. When the cue occurs, take a few soothing rhythm breaths and turn your mind back to the present moment. What is happening right now?

DAY 2: Can You Observe It?

One of my favorite ACT sayings is "If you can observe it, you aren't it."

When our feelings get intense, we may try to avoid them, or feel engulfed in them. The aim of self-compassion is to be sensitive to your feelings, *and* to stay centered enough to care for them effectively. Today you're going to practice observing your inner experience from a distance. By stepping back and looking *at* your emotion, not *from* it, you can begin to accept it for what it is and respond with compassion. Observing your emotions and putting them into words help you regulate them (Lieberman et al. 2007).

How often do you observe your inner world (circle one)?

Never   Every once   Daily   Multiple times
                in a while   in a day

Turn your attention inside. What physical sensations do you notice? What feelings do you notice?

_____

_____

_____

_____

_____

_____

_____

Pick one emotion or sensation and imagine you could place it on a canvas in front of you. If it were a painting with color, texture, and form, what would it look like? (Describe or draw your emotion in the space below.)

What would you name this painting?

_____

Did you notice any change in your experience when you observed it as you would a painting?

_____

_____

 **Today's practice.** When you notice an uncomfortable feeling today, instead of trying to make it go away, step back and observe it like a painting. Remind yourself that if you can observe it, you aren't it!

DAY 3: Feeling Cared For

You have been mindfully observing your inner experiences. The next step in self-compassion is to open yourself to kindness and care. When you "take in the good" of feeling cared for, you can turn compassion from an in-the-moment state into a longer-lasting trait (Hanson and Hanson 2018).

Like plants being watered, kindness perks us up.

According to Rick Hanson and Forrest Hanson, we have five types of caring experiences:

1. Being included
2. Being seen
3. Being appreciated
4. Being liked
5. Being loved

Instead of letting caring experiences pass by, let's take in the good and remember them.

Who makes you feel included, seen, and appreciated? Write about a memory when you felt most appreciated and loved.

_____

_____

_____

_____

_____

_____

Looking back on your week, when did you experience kindness from a person, an animal, or the environment around you? It could've been something small, like a person holding the door for you (being included), a smile (being seen), or your pet's enthusiastic welcome home (being appreciated). Or it could be something big, like a friend offering support (being loved). If you can't remember something kind done toward you, consider something you did for someone else. *Being* caring feels good, too!

_____

_____

_____

_____

_____

Consciously savoring kindness enhances our overall well-being (Smith and Bryant 2017). Pause and take a few soothing rhythm breaths and savor the good feeling of being cared for. What do you notice?

_____

_____

_____

_____

_____

Today's practice. Look out for kindness. When you notice it, savor it. Let the kindness water you and perk you up.

DAY 4: Just Like You

There's a beautiful diversity amongst humans—and there's common humanity. We all want to be happy and we all struggle. Seeing the fundamental ways in which we're similar can foster belonging. When we see our shared experience, we find strength in the greater fabric of our humanity.

Once, at the airport, I sat next to a mother scrolling on her phone while her child kept tapping her arm. I felt increasingly judgmental: *What bad parenting!* Then I heard the mom say, "Honey. We've been traveling for twelve hours. I need a break." My judgment quickly transformed to compassion. Later that week, I was working on a stressful project and snapped at my son. I remembered the mom at the airport and that we're all perfectly imperfect.

It's comforting to know, when you're struggling, that you're not unique. Whether you're going through a stressful time or made a big blunder, there's nothing wrong with you for feeling what you do. There are undoubtedly others right now who feel the same way. That's the human experience.

Reflect on the countless others who are going through something that's hard. Imagine you could talk to someone who's going through something similar. What would you tell them? What would you want to hear back?

_____

_____

_____

_____

_____

_____

Consider someone you love who's having a hard time. Just like you, they want to be free from their struggle. What would you tell them?

_____

_____

_____

_____

_____

_____

_____

_____

Today's practice. Remind yourself that your struggles can be a gift of connection. When you greet others today, can you see that in some ways they are just like you?

DAY 5: A Compassionate Perspective

This week you've been learning the three cornerstones of self-compassion: mindfulness, kindness, and common humanity. They can be especially helpful when you experience a painful event or feel badly about yourself. With mindfulness you become aware of your experience, with kindness you turn toward your experience with warmth, and with common humanity you feel less alone.

Today you'll put your compassionate perspective to work with an experience that involved failure, humiliation, or rejection. This exercise is adapted from a research study conducted by Leary et al. (2007) showing that self-compassion can help attenuate your reaction to negative events.

Think about a recent experience that made you feel bad about yourself. Describe what happened, who was present, and what led up to the event.

_____

_____

_____

_____

_____

_____

Mindfulness: Imagine you could observe yourself and your feelings from a distance. What would you see? How would you describe your feelings about the event?

_____

_____

_____

Kindness: Imagine that you had a good friend or child who had undergone the same experience. If you were to express kindness or concern toward them, what would you say?

_____

_____

_____

Common Humanity: Do you think other people have experienced similar events? How? Do you think someone is feeling something similar right now? List some ways.

_____

_____

_____

Did taking a compassionate perspective on this event change your perspective on yourself? How?

_____

_____

_____

_____

🔘 **Today's practice.** If you have a painful experience today, see if you can bring these three pillars of self-compassion to that experience. What does it make possible?

For a powerful visualization exercise on perspective taking with compassion, visit the website for this book at http://www.newharbinger.com/53496.

DAY 6: Your Compassionate Self

When Maria was diagnosed with breast cancer, she wanted to block it out. She didn't want to tell her young kids about the "C" word and avoided thinking about the part of her body that harbored cancerous cells. We practiced soothing rhythm breathing together in session. I encouraged her to imagine a wise, loving, courageous version of herself. Ever so gently, she placed her hand at her chest. As she did this, she felt a new sense of peace.

If you could have an ideal compassionate version of yourself show up for you when you needed it most, what would they be like? Take a moment to write down the qualities of your ideal compassionate self. What kind of insights or strengths would they have?

_____

_____

_____

_____

_____

_____

What is your compassionate self's facial expression like? What is their posture like? How do they sound?

_____

_____

_____

_____

_____

_____

Take a few soothing rhythm breaths. Imagine you could step into the body
of this compassionate version of you. Breathe the way they would breathe,
take on their facial expression. Silently say your name in the tone of your
compassionate self. Become this compassionate self. From this perspective,
offer yourself some wisdom about your life right now.

_____

_____

_____

_____

_____

_____

_____

Today's practice. When difficult feelings show up for you today, take on
the facial expression, posture, tone, and breath of your ideal compassionate
self.

DAY 7: Feeling Content

Today you're going to strengthen your compassionate self by adding the balancing quality of equanimity. One of the four immeasurables (qualities we can't have too much of) in Buddhist psychology, equanimity is your capacity to stay centered, content, and grounded, even during difficulty (Jinpa 2015). (The other qualities are compassion; loving-kindness—love with no strings attached; and sympathetic joy—experiencing happiness for someone else's happiness). Equanimity is like the waters deep under the ocean that are still even during a storm. Equanimity is the feeling of inner peace.

Where do you feel most content and at peace? Do you have a "safe place"? Describe it.

_____

_____

_____

_____

_____

_____

_____

_____

_____

Who helps you feel grounded and loved as you are?

_____

_____

_____

What activities help you feel balanced and whole?

_____

_____

_____

_____

Breathe in feelings of contentment and peace. Imagine you're satisfied with this moment exactly as it is. Does it change your perspective?

_____

_____

_____

_____

● **Today's practice.** Practice cultivating equanimity today. When you notice yourself getting caught up in rushing, stress, or a strong emotion, imagine a person or place that helps you feel at peace. Let yourself be bolstered by contentment.

Reflection

This week you explored the three components of self-compassion: *mindfulness*, *kindness*, and *common humanity*. You embodied your ideal compassionate self and strengthened it with the grounded feeling of equanimity. Which of this week's skills were most helpful to you? Which ones do you want to keep practicing?

_____

_____

_____

_____

_____

_____

_____

_____

_____

_____

_____

_____

_____

_____

_____

_____

Defusing from Your Inner Critic

We all have a running commentary in our heads. Sometimes our thoughts are helpful, but often they are downright mean.

Here are some common self-critical thoughts:

- *That was stupid*
- *I don't fit in*
- *It's my fault*
- *I am ugly/lazy/weak/fat*

What are some of your stickiest self-critical thoughts? Are they about your looks? Your performance? Your past? What does your mind tell you over and over?

_____

_____

_____

_____

_____

_____

Unfortunately, the mind can be the most self-critical when we are learning a new skill, stepping out of our comfort zone, or when we've made a mistake or lapsed into unhealthy old habits. Many people use self-criticism to motivate themselves to behave better, but the opposite often happens. When you belittle yourself, you're more likely to:

- Feel shame, anxiety, and depression
- Give up sooner on difficult tasks
- Be less motivated to try again
- Block learning and growth
- Be perceived by others as functioning poorly (Powers and Zuroff 1988)

You may tend to fight back against your critic, think positive thoughts, or "try not to think" negative ones. ACT and self-compassion offer a different approach. Instead, you can:

- Notice your thoughts without being caught in them
- Get some space from your self-critic
- Let your thoughts come and go
- Choose more compassionate thoughts

Choosing compassionate thoughts doesn't mean that you let yourself off the hook, inflate your ego, or allow yourself to do things that are harmful to yourself or others. Rather, it's stepping back from your automatic thoughts and responding in a new way.

This week you'll explore where your inner critic came from, learning creative ways to get space from unhelpful thoughts and turn toward more compassionate ones.

DAY 1: The Origins of Your Inner Critic

If our inner critic is so unhelpful, why do we have one? This internal voice develops for many different reasons.

Brain: Your brain evolved to avoid danger (Gilbert and Woodyatt 2017), and to use language to solve problems and plan for the future. Your brain also has a strong drive to belong to a group. But these amazing capacities can lead us to overfocus on the negative, get caught in worry, and compare ourselves to others.

What do you notice about your brain's unhelpful tendencies?

_____

_____

_____

_____

Learning History: Were your caregivers, teachers, and coaches punitive, neglectful, or punishing? Did they model perfectionism or self-criticism? You may have internalized these voices as your own.

How did you learn to be self-critical?

_____

_____

_____

_____

Culture: We live in a society that privileges certain traits, characteristics, and abilities, and discriminates against others. If you're a person of color or have other identities that are marginalized, you may have internalized these biases or learned to be self-critical for your own survival. In individualistic cultures, competition is also prioritized over collaboration, making it difficult or even dangerous to show vulnerabilities.

How has culture influenced how you relate to yourself?

_____

_____

_____

_____

Behavior: How you respond to self-critical thoughts can strengthen or weaken them. If you follow your inner critic's rules, its voice gets stronger over time.

What do you do when the critic shows up?

_____

_____

_____

_____

When you consider the larger context that created your inner critic, does it change your perspective?

_____

_____

_____

🌑 **Today's practice.** Notice your self-talk. Pause and ask yourself, *Where did this voice come from?*

DAY 2: Noticing Thoughts

Your ears hear, your eyes see, and your mind thinks! Some thoughts are one-sided (*I'm a complete failure*), some are perfectionistic (*I need to get this just right*) and some are helpful to the task at hand (*This might work better if I tried it another way*). As you learned yesterday, many of your thoughts don't even come from you in the first place.

To defuse from unhelpful thoughts, start by just noticing them. For example, while writing this book, I had two critics in my head: one telling me I wasn't getting ACT "right" and the other saying I wasn't getting compassion "right." The more I listened to those critics, the more fear, anxiety, and shame I felt and the less motivated I was to keep writing. Just noticing *That's my ACT critic* and *That's my compassion critic* helped me continue to put words on the page.

How about you? Do you have inner critics that are one-sided, perfectionistic, or shaming? Do you have more than one? What are they saying to you today?

_____

_____

_____

_____

What happens when you listen to your inner critic(s) and follow their lead?

_____

_____

_____

_____

Choose one critical thought you tend to have. Can you hear it in your head? What is its tone? Does it remind you of someone?

_____

_____

_____

_____

_____

_____

_____

When are your critical thoughts loudest? What contexts trigger them?

_____

_____

_____

_____

_____

_____

_____

_____

_____

🌓 **Today's practice.** Notice your inner critic today. Remember that your inner critic is not necessarily right and that you don't have to listen to what it says.

DAY 3: Fun with Thoughts

Another way to get space from critical thoughts is to not take them so seriously. Getting playful with your thoughts helps you see them for what they are...just words, sounds, and images that your mind creates. Instead of changing thoughts or fighting them, you could try:

- Repeating your critical thought ten times as fast as you can until it turns into gibberish
- Singing your thoughts as if you were an opera singer
- Imagining your thoughts are bad news radio in the background

In ACT, we call this practice of holding your thoughts lightly *cognitive defusion*.

Let's get playful with your thoughts right now:

Write down a critical or unhelpful thought you've had recently:

_____

Now, write the thought in bubble letters:

Write the thought in another language (pig Latin counts):

_____

_____

Write the thought as tiny as you can: _____

Write the thought with your nondominant hand:

_____

_____

What happens to the thought when you play with it in this way?

_____

_____

_____

_____

_____

_____

_____

_____

_____

_____

_____

_____

Today's practice. Today, when you notice a critical or unhelpful thought, get playful with it. Imagine writing the thought in bubble letters across your mind, then let it float by...

DAY 4: Unsticking Thoughts

Some thoughts are stickier than others. For example, I often have the thought that I suck at podcasting, and when I believe it, I overedit. I now keep sticky notes by my computer, write down self-critical thoughts when they show up, and set them aside. With a little distance from them, I can keep putting my voice into the world.

You can't permanently turn your mind off (nor would you want to) but you can step back from it and choose not to let every thought shape your behavior.

Get out a pile of sticky notes or slips of paper. Write down some of your self-critical thoughts—one thought per note.

Then, hold the thought papers up to your face. How well can you keep journaling when your thoughts are in the way? Now, place the thought papers in your lap. How well can you journal now?

_____

_____

_____

When you defuse from your thoughts, you aren't throwing them away, you're making space so you can put your attention on what's most important to you right now.

Are self-critical thoughts getting in the way of doing what you care about? How?

_____

_____

_____

Which thoughts do you want to place at a distance today?

_____

_____

_____

● **Today's practice.** Pay attention to your thoughts today. If you notice a self-critical thought, imagine writing it down on a sticky note and placing it in your lap. At the end of the day, come back to the journal to reflect. What was it like?

_____

_____

_____

_____

_____

_____

_____

_____

_____

_____

_____

_____

(For more on unsticking thoughts, try the "both/and thinking" exercise on the website for this book: http://www.newharbinger.com/53496.)

DAY 5: Choosing Helpful Thoughts

In general, a wandering mind is an unhappy mind—especially if it is wandering to unpleasant things (Killingsworth and Gilbert 2010). You may not be able to prevent mind wandering, but you can practice catching yourself when you're doing it, and shift your attention back to the here and now.

Deliberately attending to the present moment with gratitude can benefit your outlook and mood overall. When a group of students were asked to write a few sentences about gratitude for ten weeks, they were more optimistic and felt better about their lives compared to participants who wrote about daily irritations or events of the day (Emmons and McCullough 2003).

So: When your mind wanders to dread, threat, or self-criticism, catch it, and encourage it to wander to more helpful places like what you're grateful for right now.

Write a gratitude letter to yourself. Right now, what are you grateful for in your life? What are you grateful for about yourself? What changes are you making that you want to thank yourself for? How are you growing? What personal strengths are you grateful for?

Dear _____ (name),

_____

_____

_____

_____

_____

_____

_____

_____

_____

_____

_____

_____

_____

_____

In gratitude,

Me

⬤ **Today's practice.** When you notice your mind wandering, turn your mind to the present moment. Is there something to be grateful for in the here and now, including you?

DAY 6: Choosing Encouraging Thoughts

As a mom to two baseball players, I have observed a lot of great and not-so-great coaching over the years. I have also observed that by the time a player is up to bat, they're left with only one coach...themself.

What words are most motivating to you? What words center you? What helps you feel strong enough to do hard things? What kind of coach do you want to be for yourself? Today you're going to generate some encouraging self-statements that you can use in important domains of your life.

Think about your favorite coaches, teachers, and inspirational leaders. Who were they? What were their qualities?

_____

_____

_____

_____

_____

_____

_____

_____

_____

_____

_____

_____

What are some of the things they said to you that were most helpful?

_____

_____

_____

_____

_____

_____

_____

If you could imagine a coach that is encouraging and kind, who wants the best for you now, what would they say?

_____

_____

_____

_____

_____

_____

_____

_____

● **Today's practice.** Turn to your encouraging inner coach today when you need some help.

DAY 7: Watering Compassionate Thoughts

You learned this week how to step back and defuse from your thoughts, take them less seriously, and pay more attention helpful, encouraging thoughts. Your compassionate self is like a gardener who can help you choose the seeds you want to plant in your life and who waters them every day with your attention and actions. Your compassionate gardener waters your relationship seeds, work seeds, and health seeds with encouragement and wisdom.

There are many other seeds in the garden of your mind as well, some of them self-critical weeds! But why water the weeds with your attention? Today you're going to choose compassionate thoughts to water the seeds you really want to grow.

What do you want to grow in your life? What seeds need watering?

_____

_____

_____

_____

_____

_____

What compassionate thoughts would water those seeds?

_____

_____

_____

_____

_____

_____

_____

_____

Which thoughts do you want to stop watering? How could you do that?

_____

_____

_____

_____

_____

_____

_____

_____

_____

_____

● **Today's practice.** When you find yourself being critical, judgmental, or demotivating today, ask yourself, _Is this a seed I want to water?_

Reflection

We all have sticky self-critical thoughts. This week you took a step back from your inner critic, looked at where it came from, and began to get space from it. You learned a few skills to help: *defusing from thoughts, choosing helpful and encouraging thoughts,* and *watering compassionate thoughts* in your mind's garden.

Of the cognitive defusion techniques, which ones worked the best for you?

_____

_____

_____

_____

_____

_____

_____

_____

_____

_____

_____

_____

_____

_____

Opening Up and Being With

Sometimes being kind to yourself is doing hard things. I have a dental phobia that stems from my history of bulimia. Going to the dentist brings up feelings of shame and fear. Self-compassion isn't canceling or pushing off the appointment. Self-compassion is reminding myself that I am caring for my body by going, asking for support, and accepting my painful past when it shows up in the present.

We all have parts of ourselves that we don't like, experiences we avoid, or things we don't want to accept. This week you'll use the ACT core process of acceptance to face the things you cannot change and free up your energy to change the things you can. As you'll discover, opening up to the parts of ourselves we don't like gives us energy to do the things that matter most.

There's a central premise of ACT: *Pain and values are two sides of the same coin* (Hayes 2019). When you consider the relationships, work projects, or social causes that are most important to you, they're also often what make you the most sad, worried, or angry. To be your best self in these important domains, you'll likely need to open up to be with the pain that comes with them.

The root of the word acceptance is "to receive" and the ACT process of acceptance helps you "receive" difficult experiences with softness, warmth, and care. Acceptance lets you face painful emotions and sensations with courage so you can do the hard work of living from your values.

You don't have to like it to accept it. For example, when people with chronic pain willingly accept their physical discomfort, they have lower pain intensity, anxiety, and depression, and are more active in their day (McCracken 1998). Similarly, willingness to experience traumatic memories and thoughts is associated with *less* post-traumatic stress (Hayes 2019).

Acceptance is especially useful for tough things that you cannot control or change. When you stop fighting reality, you become more resilient to stress (Epel 2022) and have more energy to put toward meaningful pursuits.

DAY 1: Accept or Change?

One common place people get stuck is trying to control things they cannot control—and not taking action where they could make a difference. According to Dr. Elissa Epel, author of *The Stress Prescription*, "control is a mixed bag" (2022, 29). Feeling in control is associated with better emotion regulation, less anxiety, and protection against stress—but when we try to control things that are out of our power, it can lead to toxic chronic stress.

Today you'll look at what you can and cannot control. You cannot control the past, other people's actions, the uncertain future, and sometimes your own feelings and sensations. You *can* control how you respond when those experiences show up.

Take a moment to think of one of your top life stressors. What is it?

_____

_____

_____

Which parts of this stressor can you not control?

_____

_____

_____

_____

_____

_____

As you experience the factors you can't control, you'll notice feelings, thoughts, and sensations arise. Which of these are you willing to accept?

_____

_____

_____

_____

_____

_____

How do you want to respond when this stressor shows up? What is in your control?

_____

_____

_____

_____

_____

_____

⬤ **Today's practice.** When faced with a stressor ask yourself, _What can and can't I control here? What am I willing to accept?_

DAY 2: Softening and Letting Go

Our instinct is to resist things we don't like by holding the breath, clenching the jaw, or avoiding thinking about them. Nonacceptance takes a lot of effort and can cause more tension.

Softening around the edges of discomfort helps free you to do what you want to do, even if the discomfort doesn't go away.

Let's practice softening and letting go with a simple yoga pose.

- Stand up holding your journal so you can still read it. (You can also do this in a chair with your legs outstretched.)
- With slightly bent knees, slowly fold forward keeping your chest open.
- Stop when you notice tightness. Notice urges to grip or resist the discomfort.
- Breathe into and around the sensation, soften around it. Give it permission to be there.
- If you notice the sensation soften in response, move a bit further forward into the pose, again stopping when you find the edge of intensity. Breathe into and be open to the sensation, soften around it, and let go.
- If you wish, deepen into the pose, softening and letting go.

What did you notice?

_____

_____

_____

_____

You can apply this same principle to emotional challenges. Bring to mind something that is difficult in your life. Then make space for any feelings that show up, soften around any discomfort, and let go.

What happens?

_____

_____

_____

_____

What do you want to soften your grip around today?

_____

_____

_____

_____

_____

_____

_____

_____

_____

_____

_____

● **Today's practice.** When you notice tension or resistance, practice breathing into it and around it, softening, and letting go.

DAY 3: Offering Warmth and Support

Feeling supported can make a challenging experience more bearable. For example, when research participants held their partners' hand while anticipating a shock, they reported fewer subjective feelings of threat and showed less activation in brain areas associated with emotional responding (Coan et al. 2017).

You don't even need to have a person physically present to gain the benefits of feeling supported. For example, seeing pictures of loved ones can reduce your experience of pain (Master et al. 2009; Younger et al. 2010). Being reminded of an attachment figure when you're feeling left out seems to buffer the brain's response to social exclusion (Karremans et al. 2011).

You can practice generating feelings of warmth and support with an exercise called "the jelly roll" that I learned from meditation teacher Trudy Goodman. It's sweet and warm!

Imagine you could make a circle around you of people, pets, or spiritual figures that care for you and are happy when you do well. Who would be in that circle? Write their names in the circle on the following page.

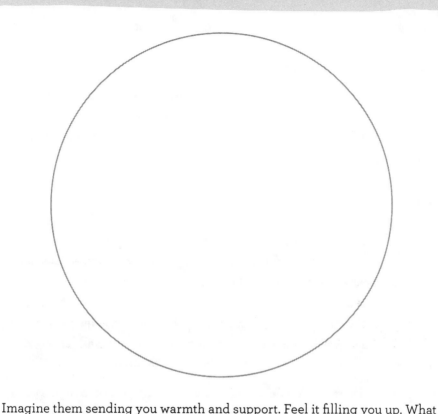

Imagine them sending you warmth and support. Feel it filling you up. What do they say to you?

_____

_____

_____

_____

_____

_____

🌑 **Today's practice.** When faced with a challenge or stressor, remember this feeling of being cared for. Imagine your jelly roll of loved ones, spiritual figures, and pets. Let the sweet warmth fill your whole body.

DAY 4: Accepting Anxiety

It's normal to have anxiety creep into your daily life—anxiety about not being liked or things going wrong. Unlike fear, which is a response to an actual threat (my friend is mad at me), anxiety is your response to a *possible* future threat (what if they get mad at me?).

Anxiety is uncomfortable and it's common to try and make it go away by avoiding what's causing it (I just won't call them back) or worrying about it (what if I say the wrong thing?).

But avoiding what makes you anxious only makes anxiety grow stronger and can lead you to miss out on what you care about. What's more, worrying doesn't prepare you any better for future events. For example, when researchers had chronic worriers record their worries for ten days, 91 percent of their worries did not come true (LaFreniere and Newman 2020)!

What can do you do instead of avoiding or worrying? Make space for anxious thoughts and feelings with curiosity and courage.

Bring to mind something you're anxious about. What worry thoughts come up in response?

_____

_____

_____

_____

_____

_____

_____

_____

Where do you feel anxiety in your body? What is it like?

_____

_____

_____

_____

Take a few soothing rhythm breaths. If you were to make space for this feeling, how big would it need to be? The size of this room? This building? This country? With each breath, breathe out more space.

_____

_____

_____

Get curious. Is your worry related to something that's important to you? What does this worry tell you about what you care about?

_____

_____

_____

_____

_____

_____

Today's practice. Notice when anxiety shows up. Instead of avoiding it or getting caught in worry, notice where you feel it in your body, make space for it, and get curious—is it pointing to something you care about?

DAY 5: Accepting Sadness

We experience mini and big losses every day. In the book *The Wild Edge of Sorrow* (2015), psychotherapist Francis Weller writes about five gates of grief we all pass through:

1. Everything we love, we will lose: we will grow old, change jobs, lose people we care about

2. The places that have not known love: we have parts of ourselves that were not cared for by others, or by ourselves

3. The sorrows of the world: we feel the pain of discrimination, war, poverty, and damage to our planet

4. What we expected and did not receive: we grieve the love we didn't get or the opportunities we didn't receive

5. Ancestral grief: we carry the trauma and hardship of our family members and heritage

Weller recommends the best way to navigate grief is to become "an apprentice" and learn from it.

Take a few soothing rhythm breaths. Which of the gates ring true for you right now?

_____

_____

_____

_____

_____

Consider the grief you wrote about above. Where do you feel it in your body? What's it like to make some space for it?

_____

_____

_____

_____

_____

_____

What have you learned from this gate of grief? Has it taught you anything about yourself or what matters to you?

_____

_____

_____

_____

_____

_____

_____

_____

● **Today's practice.** Pay attention to big or small losses today. Make space for sadness and hold it with compassion.

DAY 6: Accepting Anger

Anger is another uncomfortable human emotion. We get angry when we don't get what we want, when we feel we need to defend ourselves, or we want to fight for or protect someone or something that really matters to us.

Anger isn't inherently bad; it's what you do with it that matters. Dr. Larry Ward, author of *America's Racial Karma,* described anger as "a legitimate and genuine and precious source of information about our human experience" (2022).

You might think of your anger as a thermometer that moves from yellow to orange to red. When it's red, you might act in ways that you don't like—but your compassionate mind can help you slow down and observe your experience before it gets to that level. This way, you can really use anger as a source of information.

Try these five steps next time you experience anger:

1. Notice anger is rising
2. Practice soothing rhythm breathing
3. Bring softness and care to the part of you that is angry
4. Ask, *What does this anger tell me about what I care about?*
5. Act from that care

How do you respond to anger? Do you express it in ways you don't like? Do you suppress it?

_____

_____

_____

_____

_____

Consider something you're angry about. Try the five steps to approaching anger. What do you notice?

_____

_____

_____

_____

_____

_____

_____

_____

_____

_____

_____

_____

_____

_____

_____

_____

🌑 **Today's practice.** Look out for anger today. When it rises, practice soothing rhythm breathing, soften around it, and ask, *What's important here?*

DAY 7: Accepting Shame

Often when clients enter therapy, they say things like, "I've never told anyone this before but…" and "I'm scared if people see this part of me, they won't like me." Shame is a painful whole-body experience that everyone has sometimes. It evolved to protect us from being excluded or rejected by others, and often we respond to it by hiding aspects of ourselves. Shame can lead us to believe that some parts of us are ugly, unwanted, or unlovable.

Research shows that self-compassion is a powerful antidote to shame (Matos 2023). With self-compassion you turn toward the parts that you fear are inadequate and offer them understanding and support.

Take a few soothing rhythm breaths. Recall an early memory where you experienced shame. What happened? What does it feel like in your body when you remember this?

_____

_____

_____

_____

_____

Embody the posture, facial expression, and motive of your most compassionate self. Imagine this self could go back and support you during that time. What would you do and say?

_____

_____

_____

_____

_____

What about now? When does shame pop up?

_____

_____

Using your compassionate self, turn toward shame feelings in your body.
How can your compassionate self help you with this feeling?

_____

_____

_____

_____

_____

_____

_____

_____

● **Today's practice.** Notice pings of embarrassment or shame today.
Soften around the feeling in your body and offer your compassion. Can you
welcome this part too?

If you'd like to take compassion one step further and learn about the
practice of Tonglen meditation for difficult emotions, you can download an
extra exercise at http://www.newharbinger.com/53496.

Reflection

This week you learned how to use acceptance and willingness to turn toward difficult feelings. Which skills—*acceptance; compassionate memory;* and *bringing warmth, space, and support to what's difficult*—were the most helpful to you? Which ones are you mostly likely to keep practicing?

_____

_____

_____

_____

_____

_____

_____

_____

_____

_____

_____

_____

_____

_____

_____

_____

A Life Well Lived

Your values—not goals, not morals, but your own freely chosen intentions about how to be—are your direction in life. They guide your actions in every domain of life: relationships, work, parenting, and so on.

When you explore your values, you may discover that compassion is a value that emerges naturally when you ask yourself, *How do I want to be in the world?* If you're living in a way that doesn't match your values, you may feel disconnected, aimless, or regretful. When you're living your values, you feel more centered, and compassion flows more easily.

Knowing and acting from your values lead you, like a compass, to a life well lived. Researchers Oishi and Westgate (2022) suggest that such a life has three components:

1. **Hedonic Happiness:** experiencing pleasure, comfort, and security

2. **Meaning:** feeling like you're making a difference

3. **Psychological richness:** having interesting experiences that stretch your perspective

Living your values does not always increase hedonic happiness; it can be quite uncomfortable at times. Instead, values-based living builds the deeper components of a life well lived—meaning and psychological richness. Values offer the motivation to be of service and step out into the interesting unknown.

This week you're going to look at what it means to you to live a life well lived, so that when it comes to an end, you can say, "That was fun. I made a difference. And, what an interesting journey!"

DAY 1: Happiness, Meaning, and Psychological Richness

The only person who will be with you your whole life is you. At the end of your life, how would you like to have spent your time? What does a well-lived life mean to you? Only you really know. Today you're going to personalize your definition of well-being.

Let's look at the three components of a well-lived life:

1. *Hedonic Happiness:* What brings you pleasure? Has pursuing feeling good ever lead you offtrack from your values?

   _____

   _____

   _____

2. *Meaning:* What gives you a sense of purpose? When do you feel like you're making a difference?

   _____

   _____

   _____

3. *Psychological richness:* When do you feel like you're growing and learning the most? What sparks your curiosity and interest?

   _____

   _____

   _____

What type of person do you want to be in the world? Generous? Courageous? Curious? How do you want so show up for yourself and others? List some values you want to embody in your life well lived.

_____

_____

_____

_____

_____

_____

_____

_____

_____

_____

_____

Today's practice. To increase happiness today, savor pleasurable experiences, but don't cling to them. To increase meaning today, focus on being of service. To increase psychological richness today, do something novel and out of the ordinary. If you like, you can even do all three.

DAY 2: Self-Compassion vs. Self-Esteem

Self-compassion often gets confused with self-esteem. Valuing yourself doesn't mean boosting your ego or seeing yourself as better than others. Rather, it's believing that everyone is worthy of being included, respected, and loved—*including you.*

We build up our self-esteem and ego to shield ourselves from self-criticism, telling ourselves, *I am smart, I am beautiful, I am special.* And often, that can help us feel a bit better. However, research shows that high self-esteem has downsides. It's associated with narcissism, and often it doesn't hold up when you fall from the top or are deemed "average" (Neff 2011).

When you're high in self-compassion, on the other hand, you're more willing and motivated to change personal weaknesses, make amends when you do wrong, and try again after a failure (Breines and Chen 2012).

Self-compassion isn't being saccharine or always positive. It's valuing your well-being enough to confront behavior that needs improvement and kindly picking yourself up when you fall down.

When do you try to be better than others? How is it working?

_____

_____

_____

_____

_____

_____

_____

_____

Where can you let go of competition and focus on being the best version of yourself instead?

_____

_____

_____

_____

_____

_____

_____

_____

_____

_____

Today's practice. Value yourself as you are while encouraging yourself to grow. Notice that you're no more or less deserving of care than others. Let go of having to be the best and rest in self-compassion.

DAY 3: Whom Do You Envy?

I had a work colleague I really envied. She was great at time management and bold in asking for what she needed. My jealousy made it uncomfortable to be around her. Since I was practicing ACT, I decided to look at how my discomfort pointed to my values and saw that what I envied were qualities I wanted to embody myself— organization, prioritization of time, assertiveness. By tracing my envy back to my values, I shifted my focus to where I had agency. How could I be more intentional with my time? Where could I be bolder?

Throughout this journal, you've explored the benefits of turning toward emotions. Not only is fighting them futile, sometimes they harbor important information. For instance, what you envy in others tells you a lot about what you value. Once you uncover that latent value, you can start putting it to play in your life.

Whom do you envy?

_____

What qualities does this person have?

_____

_____

_____

_____

_____

How do those qualities point to your values?

_____

_____

_____

_____

_____

_____

How could you embody some of those values in your life today?

_____

_____

_____

_____

_____

_____

Today's practice. Take action to practice some of the values you wrote about today. If envy arises, can you dig deeper to see what values or aspirations your envy might speak to?

DAY 4: Relationship Values

One place where we can lose track of caring for ourselves is in our relationships with others. You might find that you tend to neglect your needs, have difficulty asserting yourself, or let your boundaries get crossed.

Sometimes we do these things to preserve a relationship or keep the peace. But it's valuing both yourself and the other person that allows you to have healthy relationships. For example, in *Fierce Self Compassion* (2021), Kristen Neff shares that there is extensive research showing that caregivers who are more self-compassionate are more resilient, more engaged and fulfilled, and more confident in their ability to provide calm, compassionate care to others.

And as Nedra Tawwab, author of *Set Boundaries, Find Peace*, said to me on my *Your Life in Process* podcast (2022), "I'm not setting the boundary as a way to leave the relationship. I'm setting the boundary as a way to stay in the relationship."

How do you want to act toward others in relationships?

_____

_____

_____

_____

How do you want to act toward yourself in relationships?

_____

_____

_____

_____

Choose one relationship to write about. Are there boundaries you want to set? Where do you want to be more flexible? What other values do you want to demonstrate?

_____

_____

_____

_____

_____

_____

_____

_____

What difficult emotions are you willing to accept to stay true to your values in this relationship?

_____

_____

_____

_____

_____

_____

_____

● **Today's practice.** Practice living your values in a relationship today. Notice what it feels like to care for yourself as much as you care for others.

DAY 5: Valuing at Work

How do you feel about work and your career? Workplace burnout has been on the rise since the COVID pandemic, and many workers are questioning their career paths as a result (American Psychological Association 2021).

Burnout at work isn't a given; it comes on when we work for a long time in a situation that isn't meeting our needs. Christina Maslach, a pioneer in workplace burnout, has a useful metaphor: "A pickle doesn't start out being a pickle. It starts out being a cucumber, and it's only because it's in an environment of brine that it becomes something else" (2022).

If you're feeling a little sour about work, it is likely due to one or more of these mismatches (Maslach 2022):

- *Workload:* too many demands with too few resources
- *Control:* lack of autonomy and flexibility
- *Rewards:* feeling unappreciated and unrewarded
- *Community:* feeling lack of community and belonging
- *Fairness:* experiencing inequity and discrimination
- *Values:* lacking a sense of purpose or meaning in your work

Let's figure out which of these you might be struggling with, and how to use your values to support yourself at work.

What areas are going well for you at work? When you are at your best, what does it look like?

_____

_____

_____

_____

In which of the six categories above do you feel a mismatch?

_____

_____

_____

_____

If you were to live out your values at work, how would you act? Do you
need to reduce your workload or expectations? Seek more autonomy and
flexibility? Find allies or advocates for support?

_____

_____

_____

_____

_____

_____

_____

_____

_____

Today's practice. Bring your values to work today. Notice how it
changes your outlook and performance when you care for yourself at work.

DAY 6: Valuing Your Time

Many of us feel like we don't have enough time. We rush from one thing to the next, skimming through life and not really being in it. But it may be how you relate to time, not lack of it, that's the real problem. According to Dr. Cassie Holmes, a UCLA professor who studies happiness, there's a sweet spot when it comes to time. If you have *fewer* than two hours or *more* than five hours of free time every day, you feel less happy. If you're in the extremes, you may need to free up some time or add more structure to build greater life satisfaction. But beyond those extremes, it's not how much time you have that makes a difference—it's how you spend it.

Think back to what you did yesterday. How many hours did you spend on mindless tasks (e.g., scrolling through social media) or tasks you don't enjoy (e.g., chores, commuting)?

_____

_____

Consider the three components of a life well lived. What did you enjoy doing yesterday? What was meaningful? What was most interesting and psychologically rich?

_____

_____

_____

_____

_____

_____

What was least enjoyable yesterday? What felt less meaningful? What was less interesting?

_____

_____

_____

_____

Where would you like to reallocate your time if you could? Or, if you can't, how could you make the activities you don't enjoy more meaningful and psychologically rich? For example, could you listen to podcasts while you tidy the kitchen or call a friend on your commute?

_____

_____

_____

_____

_____

🌓 **Today's practice.** Be more intentional with your time today. How could you make time more enjoyable, meaningful, and psychologically rich, no matter what you might be doing?

DAY 7: Choice Points

The term "choice point" was coined by Joseph Ciarrochi, Ann Bailey, and Russ Harris (2014) to describe the moments in our day when we have an opportunity to turn toward or away from our values.

Every day we engage in activities such as going to work, eating meals, using technology, and talking with people. Sometimes we take actions that turn us toward the type of person we want to be. Other times we turn away from the life we want to build. The good news is that every moment is a fresh opportunity to choose.

As you continue to practice self-compassion, you'll have lots of chances to make that choice to turn toward challenges with a caring and courageous heart. When you get offtrack or turn away, you can compassionately choose again.

Consider your day ahead. What situations do you anticipate might be choice points, where you could either turn toward or away from your values?

What actions would move you toward values? How could self-compassion support you in making those moves?

_____

_____

_____

_____

_____

_____

_____

_____

_____

_____

_____

_____

_____

_____

_____

_____

Today's practice. Be on alert for choice points today. In those moments, choose to turn toward the value of self-compassion.

Reflection

This week you explored what a rich and meaningful life means to you. You uncovered your *values* in relationships, work, and how you want to use your time. And you considered *choice points*—those moments in life when we can decide to act in valued ways, or not. What did you learn about yourself in exploring your values?

_____

_____

_____

_____

_____

_____

_____

_____

_____

_____

_____

_____

_____

_____

_____

_____

Compassion for Your Body

I remember being in junior high and waiting, waiting, waiting for my boobs to grow. I saw other girls getting attention for developing bodies, and I wanted that too. So one day I decided to stuff my swimsuit with toilet paper. You can imagine what happened... A boy came up behind me and dunked me, and as toilet paper wads floated to the surface, my C cup shriveled to an A minus. The things we do to fix what isn't broken!

We all have aspects of our bodies we like and aspects we don't like—maybe even those we wish we could get rid of altogether. And this can change over time.

Pause and consider your body right now. How do you feel toward it?

Aspects of my body I like: _____

_____

_____

_____

_____

_____

Aspects of my body I don't like: _____

_____

_____

_____

_____

_____

How many of the things you wrote above relate to your appearance? Having a healthy relationship with your body extends beyond looks. It includes appreciating what your body does for you, taking care to give it what it needs (food, rest, movement), and connecting to its inner wisdom. It also includes enjoying your body in relationship with others, and having compassion for the parts of it that have been neglected or harmed.

Go back and add to the list some aspects of your body that aren't appearance related—ones that speak to your values and what your body makes possible for you.

This week you'll learn to listen to your body so you can respond to its needs for food, rest, movement, and touch, and help it thrive. Caring for your body in this way is a beautiful act of self-compassion.

DAY 1: Let Your Body Talk

*I prefer to practice yoga without mirrors. My spine is crooked
from scoliosis, so my downward dog tilts to the left and my
triangle pose is more of a zigzag. Instead of worrying about how
it looks, I focus on sensing the poses from the inside. What does
alignment feel like in my body? What subtle adjustments are
needed to find my center? I let my body tell me.*

The path to body compassion isn't as simple as "just love your body." It can feel scary to connect with your body. You may not feel "at home" in your body if your external appearance doesn't match your gender identity, or if you've experienced trauma or have struggled with your body image. It can also feel challenging to befriend your body if you're experiencing illness or disability.

Body compassion isn't just body positivity. Body compassion involves "listening in" to your body's messages, caring for your body's needs, and doing what matters with the body you have now.

Write a letter to yourself from your body. What has it been like to be your body? When has that been difficult? Which body parts feel neglected? What does your body need from you?

Dear _____ (your name),

I want you to know that...

_____

_____

I appreciate it when you...

_____

_____

I feel neglected when...

_____

_____

I wish you would...

_____

_____

_____

_____

_____

Sincerely,

Your Body

● **Today's practice.** Take your body's perspective into account today. Ask your body, *What do you want and need in this moment?*

DAY 2: Interoceptive Awareness

Interoceptive awareness is your perception of physical sensations and emotions inside your body. When you learn to gently shift your attention to your body, you're better able to regulate your emotions, respond to stressors, and meet your body's physical needs. By moving your attention flexibly between your inner and outer worlds, you don't have to get stuck in uncomfortable sensations, but you don't ignore them either.

According to Price and Hooven (2018), learning interoceptive awareness has three stages. There's *body awareness*, identifying what's happening inside your body. Then, there's *accessing*, focusing inside on a specific area or sensation. Finally, there's *appraisal*, accurately interpreting and responding to your body's signals.

Let's try an interoceptive awareness exercise—one I like to call "one-eye-in, one-eye-out."

- Turn your mind's eye in to your physical body.
- What sensations do you notice? Are there sensations of hunger? Tension? Tiredness? Restlessness? Comfort? Warmth? Coolness? Pain? Just notice.
- What does your body need right now? Just listen.
- Now turn your eyes out to the world around you. What do you notice? What do you see, hear, smell?
- Finally, toggle back and forth. Turn one eye in on your body and one eye out to the world.

What did you notice when you turned one eye in?

_____

_____

_____

What did you notice when you toggled between one-eye-in and one-eye-out?

_____

_____

_____

What activities or environments help you tune in?

_____

_____

_____

_____

When would it be helpful to use the one-eye-in, one-eye-out practice today?

_____

_____

_____

_____

● **Today's practice.** Practice interoceptive awareness by practicing one-eye-in and one-eye-out.

DAY 3: Ultradian Rhythms

Every day your body goes through cycles of energy and fatigue, called *ultradian rhythms*—ultra meaning "many" and dia meaning "day" (Gerasimo 2022). By paying attention to your personal cycle of alertness versus low energy, you can better respond to your body's true needs.

When you have an energy peak, instead of fidgeting in your chair or wasting your brain power on menial tasks, try moving your body or taking on work that requires concentration, diligence, and effort. And when you have an energy dip, instead of reaching for caffeine or plopping on the couch with your phone, take a true rest: deep breathing, or a nap, nature walk, or snuggle with a pet or loved one. Practicing intermittent high-energy activity strengthens your body's stress resilience, and allowing yourself to rest when you need it supports cellular regeneration (Epel 2022).

According to Tricia Hersey, author of *Rest is Resistance: A Manifesto*, rest is also a form of reclaiming power. Many bodies, especially BIPOC bodies, have been exploited, overworked, and dehumanized by oppression. Rest is reclaiming your basic rights as a human, and it's making space to dream of a more just world.

At what times of the day do you have the most energy? When does your energy dip?

_____

_____

_____

_____

_____

_____

What do you tend to do when you feel fatigued or lose concentration? What types of ultradian breaks would you like to try instead?

_____

_____

_____

_____

_____

_____

What is most deeply restorative to you? When can you fit in a deep rest this week?

_____

_____

_____

_____

_____

_____

Today's practice. Track your energy highs and lows today. When you feel irritability, inattention, or fatigue, try a ten-minute rest. Notice its impact on your concentration and mood.

DAY 4: Compassionate Eating

Do you eat on the go, eat to soothe yourself, or forget to eat altogether? If you're shut off from your body, it can be hard to tell if you're feeling hunger or something else: stress, anger, or anxiety.

Today you're going to practice listening and responding to true hunger with compassionate eating.

Tuning in to your body's hunger cues helps you know how much to eat. Staying present while eating helps you feel nourished and know when to stop.

How do you know if you're hungry or full? What does emotional hunger versus physical hunger feel like to you?

_____

_____

_____

_____

What would you like your relationship with food to be like? What are your values around eating?

_____

_____

_____

_____

Pick one meal to eat with mindfulness and compassion today.

Before Eating: Remember your eating values. Check in with your appetite. How hungry are you? What type of food does your body need to feel nourished? Take some soothing rhythm breaths.

While Eating: Pay attention to chewing, tasting, pausing, and enjoying your food. Connect with where your food came from, the land and people that made it. Feel it nourishing your body. Notice the point of satisfaction and respect your body's signals to stop.

After Eating: Check in with your fullness. If you ate past moderate fullness, note what was happening. Did you eat for emotional reasons? Because food was available? Because you broke a food rule? What did you learn from this experience?

Write about your experience here.

_____

_____

_____

_____

_____

_____

_____

_____

_____

_____

● **Today's practice.** Practice compassionate eating for at least one meal today. How does it change your experience with eating?

DAY 5: Compassionate Movement

Despite knowing the benefits of exercise, many of us struggle to move our body as much as it wants or in the ways that it needs. Common barriers to healthy movement include unhelpful thoughts like *I'll start tomorrow*, rigid self-stories such as *Walking doesn't count*, and environmental barriers such as lack of time or access to safe places to move.

You might respond to these barriers by forcing yourself to exercise ("no pain, no gain!") or avoid moving altogether.

What are your barriers to movement? How do you respond when they show up?

_____

_____

_____

_____

_____

_____

_____

Psychological flexibility and self-compassion can help you overcome these obstacles. Research participants who receive psychological flexibility training are more likely to exercise than those who receive "exercise education" (Butryn et al. 2011). And psychological flexibility has been shown to decrease your perceived effort, increase your tolerance of discomfort, and increase your post-exercise enjoyment (Ivanova et al. 2015).

Let's use what you've learned in this journal to increase compassionate movement.

Defusion: What thoughts block you from compassionate movement? Look back at week 3 and try a defusion strategy with them.

_____

_____

Acceptance: What's most uncomfortable for you about moving your body? What unwanted experiences are you willing to make space for and accept?

_____

_____

Valuing: What's important to you about moving your body?

_____

_____

Action: What type of movement do you want to incorporate into your day today and this week?

_____

_____

_____

_____

_____

_____

🌑 **Today's practice.** Bring self-compassion and psychological flexibility to your movement. Commit to caring for your body through movement today.

DAY 6: Compassionate Touch

I have a self-compassion habit of placing my hand above my heart in difficult therapy sessions. It's my way of staying grounded in my body while staying present for my clients.

Touch is a powerful way to comfort yourself when you're hurting. You may remember the feeling of a caregiver's hand at your cheek or a loved one rubbing your back when you were little. Hugs, handholding, and even sitting side by side with someone can soothe your nervous system and tell you that you're safe.

Compassionate touch doesn't always have to come from another person. You can also practice it with yourself. Try each of these different forms of compassionate touch right now.

- Place one hand on your cheek and close your eyes for a few breaths
- Place both hands on your heart and feel it beating
- Cross your arms and give yourself a gentle squeeze
- Massage the tightness across your neck, shoulders, and upper back
- Rub your hands together then cup them over your eyes

What did you notice? Which forms of compassionate touch were most soothing for you?

_____

_____

_____

_____

What are some ways you would like to incorporate giving and receiving more touch into your day?

_____

_____

_____

_____

_____

_____

_____

_____

_____

_____

_____

_____

_____

_____

_____

_____

_____

● **Today's practice.** Pick at least one form of compassionate touch to try today. Use it during a stressful situation or a time when you want to connect more with yourself.

DAY 7: A Letter to Your Body

You began this week by listening in to your body. Your body got a chance to write you a letter on day 1, and now's your chance to write a letter back. What do you want to commit to? How can you care for your body moving forward? How do you want to incorporate some of the practices you learned:

- Interoceptive awareness
- Rest
- Compassionate Eating
- Compassionate Movement
- Compassionate Touch

Dear Body,

I am sorry I neglected you or harmed you by... _____

_____

_____

I want to listen to you when... _____

_____

_____

_____

I am learning to care for you by... _____

_____

_____

_____

My wish for you is... _____

_____

_____

_____

Love,

Me

⬤ **Today's practice.** Follow through on the commitments you made in your letter with your actions today.

Reflection

This week, you learned how to better listen to your body's needs. You learned the skills of *interoceptive awareness*, *rest*, and *compassionate eating*, *movement*, and *touch*. Through exchanging letters with your body and listening in, you might have a better sense of what your body's asking from you. What practices from this week do you want to carry forward?

Regrets and Forgiveness

I often terminate therapy with an exercise called "Appreciations, Hopes, and Regrets." Sharing appreciations and hopes with clients feels good, but it's the regrets that are the biggest teachers. "I regret not telling you sooner about my drinking," says a client. "I regret not asking about your drinking when I suspected it," I respond.

Regrets can be powerful signposts. When approached with self-compassion, regrets can guide us in making the adjustments necessary to live a meaningful life.

In the American Regret Project, Daniel Pink (2022) surveyed 4,489 people about regrets in different domains such as health, relationships, and work. His results?

- 82 percent of people say they experience regret at least occasionally
- Regret is reported to be our second most common emotion
- The only emotion mentioned more than regret was love

Reflecting on your life, what do you wish you had done differently? Where do you wish you were bolder? Which relationships do you wish you didn't let drift away? Are there unfulfilled dreams or things you wish you could change?

We all have regrets. But regret isn't all bad. It teaches us to prepare for the future, be bold, connect with others, and be moral. In fact, when faced with compassionate inquiry, regret can remind us to stay true to ourselves, make repairs, and choose differently next time.

This week you'll greet your past with curiosity and kindness, learn to uncover the values hidden under your regrets, see regret as an opportunity for growth, and stop rehashing regrets. By confronting your regrets with self-forgiveness, you can live a better life.

Day 1: What Do You Regret?

Looking back on your life, what do you wish you had done differently? Consider the four main categories of regret as outlined by Daniel Pink's research:

1. *Foundation regrets:* choosing short-term gain over long-term benefit ("I wish I'd saved more money")
2. *Boldness regrets:* not stepping up, speaking out, or showing up ("I wish I'd been truer to myself")
3. *Connection regrets:* not taking an opportunity to connect or not tending to relationships
4. *Moral regrets:* acting in ways that went against your beliefs and values (times you cheated, harmed others, or weren't loyal)

Your regrets point to your values. Turn toward your regrets with self-compassion, and use them to guide your next steps.

Foundation regrets: Do you regret not taking better care of your body, not pursuing a higher degree, not taking a chance on something? How can you act on these foundation regrets?

_____

_____

Boldness regrets: Do you regret not taking advantage of an opportunity, playing it safe, or failing to speak out or step up? Are there any bold actions you would want to take?

_____

_____

Connection regrets: Do you regret letting a relationship drift, not repairing a relationship, or failing to express how you feel? Are there any connections you want to rekindle?

_____

_____

Moral regrets: Do you regret harming others, being disloyal, cheating, dishonoring others? Are there amends you want to make?

_____

_____

What do these regrets tell you about your values?

_____

_____

_____

_____

_____

_____

_____

_____

_____

_____

● **Today's practice.** Choose one regret and take action to tend to it today.

DAY 2: It's Contextual

One of our most common thinking errors as humans is called *the fundamental attribution error*. We tend to attribute human behavior to individual characteristics and fail to recognize the role that context and environment play in our actions. Contextual and environmental factors include:

- Social support
- Financial means and access to resources
- Societal messaging
- Discrimination based on race, age, gender, sexuality, ethnicity, and ability/disability
- Biological factors, such as illness, sleep, nutrition, hormonal balance
- Traumatic experiences and early attachment

Awareness of context can help you see yourself and your regrets in a more compassionate light. For example, consider a behavior you regret. Would you have acted differently if you had more social support, more resources available to you, or more encouraging societal messaging?

Consider the regrets you wrote about yesterday. What role did context play in your actions or inaction? How did your past experiences, access to skills and resources, social network, or systemic factors like oppression impact your behavior?

_____

_____

_____

_____

_____

_____

_____

_____

_____

Does considering context change the way you view your regrets? How?

_____

_____

_____

_____

_____

🌑 **Today's practice.** Pay attention to context. How are your environment and context shaping your behavior? See yourself as part of a multifaceted system.

DAY 3: Avoiding Regrets

We naturally want to distance ourselves from the pain of past misgivings. When faced with the discomfort of regrets, we often try to avoid them ("I have no regrets," "never look backward" or "think positive") or control them (ruminating on them, intellectualizing them, or blaming ourselves).

But regrets can be a rich source of learning—if you're willing to look at them without getting stuck in them. You don't need to hide regrets away or endlessly berate yourself. Feel them and let them guide you toward change.

Consider a regret you have about your past. Let's bring some mindfulness, kindness, and common humanity to your regret, instead of avoiding it.

Write about your regret below.

_____

_____

_____

_____

_____

_____

Describe your feelings and thoughts about this regret. (I notice the feelings... I notice the thoughts...)

_____

_____

_____

_____

If you could go back and talk to yourself at the time of the actions you regret, what kind, wise words could tell yourself?

_____

_____

_____

_____

_____

If you were sitting in a circle of five other people with the same regret, what would you tell them?

_____

_____

_____

_____

_____

_____

_____

Today's practice. Notice your tendency to avoid discomfort and "move on" too quickly or your tendency to get stuck in self-blame. Is there another, more compassionate path?

DAY 4: A Spacious Heart

When you feel the pang of regret, sorrow, or defeat, you can bring mindful, loving awareness to it. As meditation teacher Jack Kornfield (2022) shares, offering yourself love, attention, kindness, and a spacious perspective in times of struggle can liberate your heart.

The week-2 practices to cultivate loving awareness can be especially helpful when it comes to our regrets. Here are three simple but powerful things to do when regret shows up:

1. Turn toward the feeling of regret in your body and offer it softness and warmth

2. Take a spacious and caring perspective

3. Ask yourself, *What is there to learn from this experience*?

What are you going through right now that could use more loving awareness?

_____

_____

_____

_____

_____

_____

Where do you feel this difficulty in your body? Describe what it feels like.

_____

_____

_____

_____

_____

Imagine creating a space big enough for this feeling. How big would it need
to be?

_____

With a caring heart ask yourself, *What is there to learn from this
experience?*

_____

_____

_____

_____

_____

_____

_____

_____

_____

_____

● **Today's practice:** Give yourself the gift of loving awareness today.
When you notice something difficult show up, step back with kindness and
ask, *What is there to learn from this experience?*

DAY 5: Sharing Regrets

Often we hide our regrets from others because we feel shame about them. And we fear rejection. But exchanging regrets with another person can be one of the best ways to get perspective on those regrets and bring relief.

Francis Weller (2015) writes that to loosen the grip of shame, we need to take three steps:

1. Shift from seeing ourselves as worthless to seeing ourselves as wounded

2. Shift from seeing ourselves through the lens of contempt to one of compassion

3. Move from silence to sharing

You have been working on shifting how you see yourself and taking a more self-compassionate perspective—one that is mindful, kind, and connected. Your next step in transforming shame and regret is to share it with someone else.

If you were to share your regrets with another person, pet, or spiritual figure, who would you want to tell?

_____

_____

_____

What would you want to tell them?

_____

_____

_____

_____

_____

_____

_____

_____

_____

_____

_____

_____

🌑 **Today's practice.** Today, share your regrets. You can share your regrets through prayer, or directly with a person, an animal, a friend, or a therapist. (Or you can share them anonymously online at https://worldregretsurvey.com.)

DAY 6: Forgiving Yourself

We naturally want to avoid feelings of shame and guilt. We push away these feelings within ourselves. But as long as you keep distance from parts of yourself, they will never get a chance to heal. With self-forgiveness we lean into the parts of ourselves we have pushed away. We learn to stay with the harm long enough for it to soften and transform.

Forgiveness is not condoning or forgetting about harm that's been done. You can forgive yourself while committing to never harm yourself or another in that way again. Forgiveness doesn't let you off the hook. Instead, you intentionally contact the harm that was done, honor it, learn from it, and give yourself the gift of beginning anew.

Forgiving yourself is an act of radical self-love that you will likely need to repeat throughout life. Learning to forgive yourself opens you to a deeper connection with yourself, and practicing forgiving yourself can make it easier to forgive people who have harmed you.

Consider something that you have had difficulty forgiving yourself for. Bringing this regret to mind, practice a few soothing rhythm breaths, and if you feel ready, try offering yourself forgiveness below.

Dear _____ (your name),

I am aware of the pain I have caused you and I feel the hurt of that pain. I ask for your forgiveness for...

_____

_____

_____

_____

Love,

Me

Dear Me,

I forgive you and release you to begin anew.

Love,

_____ (your name)

How do you feel after writing and reading this passage?

_____

_____

_____

_____

_____

_____

_____

_____

_____

_____

_____

_____

_____

Today's practice. Download and listen to the forgiveness meditation at http://www.newharbinger.com/53496.

DAY 7: The Flow of Forgiveness

Yesterday you worked on forgiving yourself. Today you'll expand that forgiveness to someone you struggle with.

Forgiveness, like compassion, can flow three ways (Gilbert and Choden 2014). There's *self-forgiveness*—giving compassion to yourself. There's *taking in forgiveness*—receiving compassion from others. And there's *offering forgiveness*—sending your compassion outward to another person or group.

With the flow of forgiveness, you soften your heart toward yourself, allow others to forgive you, and offer that forgiveness to others. Again, you're not erasing what was done, but rather acknowledging the hurt, accepting it, and letting go.

Much of forgiveness is an inside job. You do not have to have contact with the person you're forgiving or ever see or speak to them again.

Write about someone who has caused you harm. Would letting go of resentment and blame toward this person benefit you or others?

_____

_____

_____

_____

_____

Are you open to forgiving the person who caused you harm? What would that look like?

_____

_____

_____

Write about someone you have caused harm to. Would asking for forgiveness benefit you or others?

_____

_____

_____

_____

_____

Are you open to asking for forgiveness? What would that look like?

_____

_____

_____

_____

_____

● **Today's practice.** Look for opportunities to practice the flow of forgiveness today: self-forgiveness, receiving forgiveness, and giving forgiveness.

Reflection

This week you explored the uncomfortable emotion of regret and learned how to *use regret to your advantage*—as a spur to recommitting to your values. You also learned about *forgiveness* and started a lifelong practice of turning toward your and others' misgivings with *loving awareness* and compassion. How do you want to carry these lessons forward?

_____

_____

_____

_____

_____

_____

_____

_____

_____

_____

_____

_____

_____

_____

_____

Compassionate Action

Congratulations! You made it to this final week of your *Self-Compassion Daily Journal*. You've learned how to be kinder toward yourself, step back from self-critical thoughts, reconnect with your body, and open to life's discomfort with a caring heart. This week you're going to solidify these skills, turn them into daily habits, and extend your compassion outward beyond yourself.

Compassion isn't just a soothing emotion; it's also an energizing one. It can motivate us to speak up, set boundaries, or make a change (Neff 2021). Turning that motivation into a behavior that you do with your voice, hands, and feet is taking *committed action*. In ACT, committed action is the process of doing things in the direction of your values, even in the face of obstacles (Moran, Bach, and Batten 2018). With your committed action, you can make compassion a habit.

Change can be uncomfortable and scary, and require effort. Yet change is going to happen whether you like it or not, so it's wise to learn how to harness change for the better (Hayes, Ciarrochi, and Bailey 2022). A compassionate perspective can help.

The Flow of Compassion

One very hot day in Santa Barbara, my husband excitedly called me out to our beehive to take a look. A swarm of bees had gathered around the door of the hive in a triangle shape, making what is called a "bee beard." Flapping their little wings outside the door, they cooled down the comb inside so it wouldn't melt. A bee colony's survival is a group effort. They need each other to make it through life's inevitable challenges. In unison they were protecting their collective home.

If you zoom out and consider the challenges we face as humans, you're likely to see that, like bees, we depend on each other to survive. Our brains and nervous systems evolved to caretake, cooperate, and co-regulate each other. We are stronger together.

Throughout this journal you have focused on self-compassion, but your "self" extends beyond just your inner world. You have an inter-self that connects you in relationships with others, and an intra-self that connects you in relationship to our planet (Siegel 2022). Compassion can flow between and within these intra-connected selves like air, moving in, out, and between us.

Compassion flows three ways (Gilbert and Choden 2014):

1. Giving compassion to yourself

2. Receiving compassion from others

3. Offering compassion to others

Some of these are more difficult for us than others. But by entering the flow of compassion, we can navigate life's challenges more effectively, together.

DAY 1: Motivation to Act

Over the past few weeks, you've explored how your pain, including anxiety, grief, and anger, points to what matters most to you. When you contact that pain, compassion arises naturally, and this becomes your motivation to act. What keeps you up at night? What news articles worry you the most? What do you fear for yourself? What do you fear for others? What angers you? The answers to these questions are a window into your values. Today you'll explore these values to generate motivation to act outwardly with compassion.

What do you worry about for yourself? Your health? Your work? Your relationships? Your future? What do these worries tell you about how you want to care for yourself?

_____

_____

_____

_____

_____

What news articles are most distressing to you? What does this distress tell you about what you care about in relation to others or the planet?

_____

_____

_____

_____

_____

What angers you about the state of the world? What frustrates you because you believe it is unjust? What does this anger and frustration tell you about what you want to protect or make right?

_____

_____

_____

_____

Now, take the values that you wrote about above and make a list in the space below. These are the values that you're going to take committed action toward this week.

_____

_____

_____

_____

_____

_____

_____

_____

_____

_____

_____

● **Today's practice.** Pay attention to worry, anger, or feelings of unfairness today. How can this motivate you to take compassionate action?

DAY 2: Giving Compassion

The goal of this journal isn't just to make you "feel better"; it's to help you engage with life in ways that matter. Your well-being is inherently intertwined with the well-being of your family, community, and planet. Today you're going to act like a prosocial bee and expand your compassion beyond just yourself, to people and creatures in the world around you.

It's important to distinguish between empathy and compassion. Empathy is putting yourself in other people's shoes and feeling what they feel. Compassion has the extra step of pulling up your sleeves and doing what you can to relieve their suffering. It requires more effort, because it involves taking action, but it can also be deeply satisfying. And with the flow of compassion, you can also hold yourself with kindness as you help others.

What person, group, or living thing would you like to offer more compassion toward?

_____

_____

_____

What behaviors could you engage in that would enact that compassion?

_____

_____

_____

_____

_____

_____

How could you care for yourself as you do this?

_____

_____

_____

_____

_____

_____

_____

_____

_____

_____

● **Today's practice.** Offer compassion to another person or being today. Remember to hold yourself with compassion as you do it.

DAY 3: Identifying and Overcoming Barriers

We all face barriers to taking compassionate action. Inner barriers include things like thoughts, emotions, or stories about yourself and others. External barriers include obstacles like transportation, time constraints, limited resources, or risk of being harmed. Psychological flexibility is especially helpful for inner barriers, and problem-solving skills and community support can help with external barriers. Let's unpack both.

Consider a compassionate action you want to take. Write it here:

_____

Thoughts as barriers: What thoughts get in the way of this action? For example, *Nothing I can do would be big enough to make a difference.* Or *I am too busy with everyday responsibilities.*

_____

_____

_____

Go back and review week 3 on defusing from thoughts. Can you notice this thought and get playful with it? What thoughts would be more helpful to choose?

_____

_____

_____

_____

_____

Emotions as barriers: What emotions are getting in the way of taking action? For example, are you uncomfortable joining a group or afraid of failing?

_____

_____

Go back and review week 4 on acceptance. How can you use the compassion skills you've learned to support you with these feelings?

_____

_____

_____

_____

External barriers: Consider the logistical and external barriers to taking action. Do you have limited time? Limited resources? Other challenges?

_____

_____

_____

Are there creative solutions to these barriers? Whom could you ask for help in solving this problem?

_____

_____

🌑 **Today's practice.** Notice the barriers that show up when practicing compassion. Face them with psychological flexibility.

DAY 3: Make It Smaller

The mistake I typically see when people are trying to make a change is they do too much at once. New behaviors are more likely to stick if you break them down into small steps. As habit guru B. J. Fogg suggests (2021), if you want to be successful at flossing your teeth, start with flossing just one tooth. When you feel like you have that small change nailed down, you can add more.

It's also helpful to recognize motivation can wane. Will you be able to keep it up when you're tired, stressed, or irritable? How will you get back on track when you stumble? If you're prepared for imperfection, you're more likely to succeed, because no one does change perfectly.

Pick a compassionate action you want to take. Break it down into small steps. Then make it even smaller. Make sure you could still do it, even when your motivation is low.

_____

_____

_____

_____

_____

_____

_____

_____

Now, imagine yourself intending to do this but getting offtrack. How would you want to respond?

_____

_____

_____

_____

What values do you want to focus on while taking action? How can you focus on these values?

_____

_____

_____

_____

_____

_____

_____

_____

Today's practice. Take the first small step toward a change you want to make. When you do it, reinforce yourself by reminding yourself why it's important to you.

DAY 4: Receiving Compassion

The flow of compassion moves three ways: self-compassion, taking in compassion, and giving compassion to another. For many of us, taking in compassion from someone else can be a challenge. You may fear that asking for help demonstrates weakness, or that you will become dependent on others. Or you may worry that if you let others in, they will discover something bad about you that will change their opinion about you. Just as fears of self-compassion can block you from getting the support you need, fearing compassion from others can block you from opportunities for connection and care.

Do you have fears about receiving compassion? What are they?

_____

_____

_____

_____

_____

Write about a memory of a time when you received support and it was helpful.

_____

_____

_____

_____

_____

_____

If you could receive support around something this week, what would it be?

_____

_____

_____

_____

Is there a person or group you could ask for support from this week? If no one comes to mind, where could you look for support (e.g., search for a therapist, an online group, or a community program)?

_____

_____

_____

_____

_____

🌙 **Today's practice.** Notice your fears of receiving compassion and challenge them by asking for support.

DAY 5: Harmonious Habits

Habits are behaviors that become automatic over time. They're your brain's way of preserving energy and making life easier for you (Brewer 2021). Today you're going to create some compassion habits.

According to Dr. Jud Brewer, a neuroscientist at Brown University and author of *Unwinding Anxiety*, habits follow a predictable pattern:

Cue—something that triggers you to act

Behavior—the action you take

Reward—the consequence that keeps it going

How could you make compassion a habit? You encounter cues every day that are opportunities to give and receive compassion. For example, your friend texts that they're having a bad day, you make a mistake, or you're stressed at work and someone offers to help.

How do you respond when these cues show up? Making compassion a habit takes three steps:

1. Cue—pay attention to people who need care (including you)
2. Behavior—open your heart and offer or receive support
3. Reward—take in the good feeling of caring or being cared for

The reward for acting on compassion is multifold. Compassion feels good, making it a natural reinforcer; it's also contagious, influencing others to be compassionate in return.

What are some cues that could trigger your compassion habit?

_____

_____

_____

_____

_____

What behaviors could you engage in that would enact your care?

_____

_____

_____

_____

_____

What is rewarding to you about offering compassion?

_____

_____

_____

_____

_____

● **Today's practice.** Make compassion a habit today. Take in the good feeling of caring for yourself and others.

Day 6: A Compassion Ritual

Rituals bring intention to something we want to honor. They're not routines; rituals have more meaning to them and are done with mindfulness, grace, and ceremony. You can turn almost anything into a ritual. I've worked with clients who have created rituals around reading to their kids, drinking their morning tea, making soup, commuting, or going to bed. We crave repetition, and creating a compassion ritual is a beautiful way to keep a practice going.

A compassion ritual can take many forms. It might be practicing a round of soothing rhythm breathing as you start your commute, creating a rest ritual with music, sending well wishes to a person or group of people, or making an altar you visit regularly, where you keep objects that remind you that you belong. You can also use the science of habits from yesterday—using a specific time to cue your ritual, doing your behaviors in the same sequence each time, and taking in the good feelings of compassion—to create your ritual.

What compassion ritual would you like to add to your day? Describe the cues, behaviors, and rewards associated with your ritual.

_____

_____

_____

_____

_____

_____

_____

_____

_____

_____

_____

_____

_____

_____

_____

_____

_____

_____

_____

_____

🌑 **Today's practice.** Prepare your space for your compassion ritual. Gather the items needed and get it started.

Date: _____

Day 7: Your Self-Compassion Toolkit

Today is your last day of the *Self-Compassion Daily Journal*! Go back and review what you wrote about your hopes on week 1, day 1. Did some of them come true? Remember that self-compassion is a lifelong process.

Below are the self-compassion skills you have learned over the past eight weeks. Rate the skills from 0 (not helpful) to 10 (helpful) on the line next to the skill and check the boxes next to the ones you would like to go back and review.

WEEK 1 SKILLS

○ Creative hopelessness _____

○ Explore fears of compassion _____

○ Soothing rhythm breathing _____

WEEK 2 SKILLS

○ Being present _____

○ Savoring kindness _____

○ Common humanity _____

WEEK 3 SKILLS

○ Defusing from thoughts _____

○ Choosing thoughts _____

○ Watering compassionate thoughts _____

WEEK 4 SKILLS

○ Offering softness and warmth _____

○ Compassion for difficult emotions _____

WEEK 5 SKILLS

- O Living your values _____
- O Choice points _____

WEEK 6 SKILLS

- O Interoceptive awareness _____
- O Compassionate eating _____
- O Compassionate movement _____
- O Compassionate touch _____

WEEK 7 SKILLS

- O Loving awareness _____
- O Sharing regrets _____
- O Forgiveness _____

WEEK 8 SKILLS

- O Making it smaller _____
- O Giving compassion _____
- O Receiving compassion _____
- O Harmonious habits _____
- O Compassion rituals _____

Which practices were most helpful to you? Which ones are you most likely to do?

_____

_____

_____

Which ones would you like to continue?

_____

_____

_____

_____

_____

_____

And—while we don't practice compassion seeking any particular benefit—
have you felt these practices change your life in some way?

_____

_____

_____

_____

_____

_____

_____

_____

_____

● **Today's practice.** Choose at least three core self-compassion practices
that you will commit to doing after you're done with this journal. Write
them on a sticky note and put it on your mirror, or keep them in a note in
your phone as a reminder.

Reflection

As you close your last week of this journal and reflect on the new skills you learned—*giving and receiving compassion, harmonious habits,* and *rituals*—pause and breathe. What do you want to tell yourself about the work you have done here? What do you want to tell your future self about what to remember and keep practicing?

_____

_____

_____

_____

_____

_____

_____

_____

_____

_____

_____

_____

_____

_____

_____

_____

_____

_____

Your Compassionate Flow

I believe that there is a deep goodness in you, and I hope that over the course of completing this journal you've begun to see that too. At our core, we all have a natural quality of goodness and a longing to make a positive difference in the world. You've been strengthening that core over the last eight weeks. By welcoming in the parts of you that hurt, cultivating self-love, and committing to taking action with kindness, you're becoming what has already been there all along.

You began your compassion journey by looking at some of the fears you may have about being kinder to yourself. Thinking back, did your fears come true?

_____

_____

_____

_____

  I hope that you're starting to see the benefits of shifting to a kinder perspective in your mood, relationships, feelings of self-worth, and motivation.
  I also hope that you're seeing how self-compassion is a process that continues to unfold over time. There's no end point. It's normal for self-criticism to creep back in; as you've learned, "negative" experiences can't be avoided or eliminated. But now you know that when self-critical thoughts arise, you can practice the three simple steps of self-compassion:

1. *Be present:* tune in and notice with one-eye-in and one-eye-out

2. *Be kind:* offer yourself softness, warmth, and encouragement

3. *Be connected:* remember that you are not alone in your struggles

Sometimes life can feel like you're walking across a balance beam. You lose focus and fall off, you get motivated and climb back on, or you hit a hardship and need to go really slow. But no one moves forward without some wobble. It's actually the wobbling that helps you keep your balance! Self-compassion and psychological flexibility help you get back on the beam and find your balance again. When you find yourself off center, remember your self-compassion skills:

- *Creative hopelessness:* take an honest look at what's not working and be willing to try something different

- *Compassionate perspective taking:* stay present, see yourself with kind eyes and remind yourself everyone wobbles sometimes

- *Defuse from your inner critic:* step back from unhelpful thoughts that throw you off balance and choose compassionate self-talk instead

- *Open up and be with:* let go of gripping and open to your full experience, good and bad

- *Live your values:* remember what's most important to you and show up in a way that demonstrates your caring heart

- *Have compassion for your body:* listen in to your body's wisdom and respond to its needs

- *Practice forgiveness:* remember that everyone gets off balance and falls—be gentle with yourself and learn from your mistakes

- *Take compassionate action:* keep moving forward and don't forget to look up sometimes to see where you're headed, how far you have come, and that you're not alone

With these skills, you can continue to practice self-compassion no matter what obstacles show up. And like walking a balance beam, self-compassion will become easier over time with practice. But no one gets a perfect 10 all the time. Be self-compassionate with your self-compassion practice!

And if you're like many people and need some extra help along the way, you can download the Self-Compassion Daily Planner at http://www.newhar binger.com/53496.

Self-compassion is a lifelong process. May it nourish you, so you can live your fullest life and offer your greatest good to the world around you.

Acknowledgments

No one learns about compassion by themselves. This journal was a collective effort that came from many supportive, caring relationships. Thank you to Mathew McKay, who planted the seeds for this book during our self-compassion real-play at ACBS WorldCon. Thank you to New Harbinger, especially my editors, Elizabeth Hollis-Hansen, Vicraj Gill, and Joyce Wu, for staying flexible with me and making everything look and sound so much better. To my personal editor, Jess Beebe, with your keen eye and compassionate voice, and to Elizabeth Slivjak for organizing citations. Thank you to Joseph Ciarrochi for your enthusiasm, support, and generous foreword. And to Debbie Sorensen, my coauthor of *ACT Daily Journal,* who started this daily journal journey with me!

This journal is possible because of the ideas and practices developed by researchers and clinicians from compassion focused therapy and acceptance and commitment therapy. Thank you to those who paved the path—Steven Hayes, Kelly Wilson, Paul Gilbert, Joseph Ciarrochi, Marcela Matos, Dennis Tirch, Jud Brewer, Elissa Epel—and to the Association for Contextual Behavioral Science, the professional organization of ACT, which has been a source of intellectual richness and community.

Thank you to my root teacher in compassion, Thich Nhat Hanh, and my gentle and encouraging spiritual mentors who walk in his footsteps: Rick Hanson, Trudy Goodman, Jack Kornfield, Brother Phap Huu, and Gary Hill. And in gratitude for the organizations where I teach: Blue Spirit Costa Rica, Yoga Soup, InsightLA, Insight Timer, Praxis, Mindful.org and PESI Continuing Education.

Thank you to the guests on the *Your Life in Process* podcast who inspired many of these pages and to my podcast team, Craig Schneider, Ashley Hiatt, Alane Schnelkin, and Yoko Nguyen.

To my kalyāna mitta (spiritual friends): Meg McKelvie, Alexis Bachik, Rae Littlewood, Adele Kurstin, Isa Eaton, Katharine Foley Saldeña, Brianna Pettit, Kristen Ruskey, Susan McArver, Sonya Looney, and Lara Fielding—you keep me going when it's hard. I hope I do the same for you.

And to my clients. Our conversations echo through these pages. Thank you for showing me how to be courageous and strong.

And to my family. Dad, thank you for letting me earmark your books and rehash your Buddhist scholarship. Mom, your compassion for me is endless. And Ashley, thank you for being a loving big sister.

Thank you to my life partner in all things, Craig, for your unconditional love. To my boys, Walker and Henry, you are my biggest teachers in compassion.

May you know your values.

May you see your strengths.

May you act with compassion.

References

American Psychological Association. 2021. "The American Workforce Faces Compounding Pressure: APA's 2021 Work and Well-Being Survey Results." https://www.apa.org/pubs/reports/work-well-being/compounding-pressure-2021.

Breines, J. G., and S. Chen. 2012. "Self-Compassion Increases Self-Improvement Motivation." *Personality and Social Psychology Bulletin* 38(9): 1133–43.

Brewer, J. A. 2021. *Unwinding Worry: New Science Shows How to Break the Cycles of Worry and Fear to Heal Your Mind*. New York: Avery.

Butryn, M. L., E. Forman, K. Hoffman, J. Shaw, and A. Juarascio. 2011. "A Pilot Study of Acceptance and Commitment Therapy for Promotion of Physical Activity." *Journal of Physical Activity & Health* 8(4): 516–22.

Chwyl, C., P. Chen, and J. Zaki. 2021. "Beliefs About Self-Compassion: Implications for Coping and Self-Improvement." *Personality and Social Psychology Bulletin* 47(9): 1327–42. https://doi.org/10.1177/0146167220965303.

Ciarrochi, J., A. Bailey, and R. Harris. 2014. *The Weight Escape: How to Stop Dieting and Start Living*. Boston: Shambhala Publications, Inc.

Coan, J. A., L. Beckes, M. Z. Gonzalez, E. L. Maresh, C. L. Brown, and K. Hasselmo. 2017. "Relationship Status and Perceived Support in the Social Regulation of Neural Responses to Threat." *Social Cognitive and Affective Neuroscience* 12(10): 1574–83. https://doi.org/10.1093/scan/nsx091.

Emmons, R. A., and M. E. McCullough. 2003. "Counting Blessings Versus Burdens: An Experimental Investigation of Gratitude and Subjective Well-Being in Daily Life." *Journal of Personality and Social Psychology* 84(2): 377–89. https://doi.org/10.1037/0022-3514.84.2.377.

Epel, E. 2022. *The Stress Prescription: Seven Days to More Joy and Ease (The Seven Days Series)*. New York: Penguin Books.

Fogg, B. J. 2021. *Tiny Habits: The Small Changes That Change Everything*. New York: Harvest Publications.

Gerasimo, P. 2022. "How to Be a Healthy Deviant with Pilar Gerasimo." Your Life in Process (podcast), hosted by D. Hill. https://drdianahill.com/038-how-to-be-a-healthy-deviant-with-pilar-gerasimo.

Gilbert, P., and P. Choden. 2014. *Mindful Compassion: How the Science of Compassion Can Help You Understand Your Emotions, Live in the Present, and Connect Deeply with Others*. Oakland, CA: New Harbinger Publications.

Gilbert, P., K. McEwan, M. Matos, and A. Rivis. 2011. "Fears of Compassion: Development of Three Self-Report Measures." *Psychology and Psychotherapy* 84: 239–55.

Gilbert, P., and L. Woodyatt. 2017. "An Evolutionary Approach to Shame-Based Self-Criticism, Self-Forgiveness, and Compassion." In *Handbook of the Psychology of Self-Forgiveness*, edited by L. Woodyatt, E. L. Worthington, M. Wenzel, and B. J. Griffin. New York: Springer International Publishing AG.

Hanson, R., and F. Hanson. 2018. *Resilient: How to Grow an Unshakable Core of Calm, Strength, and Happiness*. New York: Harmony Books.

Hayes, L. L., J. Ciarrochi, and A. Bailey. 2022. *What Makes You Stronger: How to Thrive in the Face of Change and Uncertainty Using Acceptance and Commitment Therapy*. Oakland, CA: New Harbinger Publications.

Hayes, S. C. 2019. *A Liberated Mind: How to Pivot Toward What Matters*. New York: Avery.

Hayes, S. C., and S. Smith. 2005. *Get Out of Your Mind and Into Your Life: The New Acceptance and Commitment Therapy*. Oakland, CA: New Harbinger Publications.

Hayes S. C., K. D. Strosahl, and K. G. Wilson. 1999. *Acceptance and Commitment Therapy: An Experiential Approach to Behavior Change*. New York: The Guilford Press.

———. 2012. *Acceptance and Commitment Therapy: The Process and Practice of Mindful Change*, 2nd ed. New York: The Guilford Press.

Hersey, T. 2022. *Rest Is Resistance: A Manifesto*. New York: Little, Brown Spark.

Holmes, C. 2022. *Happier Hour: How to Beat Distraction, Expand Your Time, and Focus on What Matters Most*. New York: Gallery Books.

Ivanova, E., D. Jensen, J. Cassoff, F. Gu, and B. Knäuper. 2015. "Acceptance and Commitment Therapy Improves Exercise Tolerance in Sedentary Women." *Medicine and Science in Sports and Exercise* 47(6): 1251–8. https://doi.org/10.1249/MSS.0000000000000536.

Jinpa, T. 2015. *A Fearless Heart: How the Courage to Be Compassionate Can Transform Our Lives*. New York: Avery.

Karremans, J. C., D. J. Heslenfeld, L. F. van Dillen, and P. A. van Lange. 2011. "Secure Attachment Partners Attenuate Neural Responses to Social Exclusion: An FMRI Investigation." *International Journal of Psychophysiology* 81(1): 44–50. https://doi.org/10.1016/j.ijpsycho.2011.04.003.

Killingsworth, M. A., and D. T. Gilbert. 2010. "A Wandering Mind Is an Unhappy Mind." *Science* 330(6006): 932. https://doi.org/10.1126/science.1192439.

Kornfield, J. 2022. "The Transformative Power of Loving Awareness." Speech presented at the From Striving to Thriving Summit 2.0, October. https://drdianahill.com/from-striving-to-thriving-summit.

LaFreniere, L. S., and M. G. Newman. 2020. "Exposing Worry's Deceit: Percentage of Untrue Worries in Generalized Anxiety Disorder Treatment." *Behavior Therapy* 51(3): 413–23. https://doi.org/10.1016/j.beth.2019.07.003.

Leary, M. R., E. B. Tate, C. E. Adams, A. Batts Allen, and J. Hancock. 2007. "Self-Compassion and Reactions to Unpleasant Self-Relevant Events: The Implications of Treating Oneself Kindly." *Journal of Personality and Social Psychology* 92(5): 887–904.

Lieberman, M. D., N. I. Eisenberger, M. J. Crockett, S. M. Tom, J. H. Pfeifer, and B. M. Way. 2007. "Putting Feelings into Words: Affect Labeling Disrupts Amygdala Activity in Response to Affective Stimuli." *Psychological Science* 18(5): 421–8. https://doi.org/10.1111/j.1467-9280.2007.01916.x.

Marshall, S. L., P. D. Parker, J. Ciarrochi, B. Sahdra, C. J. Jackson, and P. C. L. Heaven. 2015. "Self-Compassion Protects Against the Negative Effects of Low Self-Esteem: A Longitudinal Study in a Large Adolescent Sample." *Personality and Individual Differences* 74: 116–21.

Maslach, C. 2022. "What to Do About Workplace Burnout with Dr. Christina Maslach." Your Life in Process (podcast), hosted by D. Hill. https://drdianahill.com/043-what-to-do-about-workplace-burnout-with-dr-christina-maslach.

———. 2022. *The Burnout Challenge: Managing People's Relationships with Their Jobs.* Cambridge, MA: Harvard University Press.

Master, S. L., N. I. Eisenberger, S. E. Taylor, B. D. Naliboff, D. Shirinyan, and M. D. Lieberman. 2009. "A Picture's Worth: Partner Photographs Reduce Experimentally Induced Pain." *Psychological Science* 20(11): 1316–8. https://doi.org/10.1111/j.1467-9280.2009.02444.x.

Matos, M. 2023. "Growing Courage, Healing Shame, and Overcoming Fears of Compassion with Dr. Marcela Matos." Your Life in Process (podcast), hosted by D. Hill. https://drdianahill.com/062-growing-courage-healing-shame-and-overcoming-fears-of-compassion-with-dr-marcela-matos.

Matos, M., K. McEwan, M. Kanovský, J. Halamová, S. Steindl, N. Ferreira, M. Linharelhos, et al. 2021. "Fears of Compassion Magnify the Harmful Effects of Threat of COVID-19 on Mental Health and Social Safeness across 21 Countries." *Clinical Psychology & Psychotherapy* 28(6): 1317–33.

McCracken, L. 1998. "Learning to Live with the Pain: Acceptance of Pain Predicts Adjustment in Persons with Chronic Pain." *Pain* 74(1): 21–7. https://doi.org/10.1016/S0304-3959(97)00146-2.

Moran, D. J., P. A. Bach, and S. V. Batten. 2018. *Committed Action in Practice: A Clinician's Guide to Assessing, Planning, and Supporting Change in Your Client.* Oakland, CA: New Harbinger Publications, Inc.

Neely, M. E., D. L. Schallert, S. S. Mohammed, R. M. Roberts, and Y.-J. Chen. 2009. "Self-Kindness When Facing Stress: The Role of Self-Compassion, Goal Regulation, and Support in College Students' Well-Being." *Motivation and Emotion* 33(1): 88–97.

Neff, K. D. 2011. "Self-Compassion, Self-Esteem, and Well-Being." *Social and Personality Psychology Compass* 5(1): 1–12.

———. 2021. *Fierce Self-Compassion: How Women Can Harness Kindness to Speak up, Claim Their Power, and Thrive.* New York: Harper Wave.

Neff, K. D., and C. Germer. 2018. *The Mindful Self-Compassion Workbook: A Proven Way to Accept Yourself, Build Inner Strength, and Thrive.* New York: The Guilford Press.

Oishi, S., and E. C. Westgate. 2022. "A Psychologically Rich Life: Beyond Happiness and Meaning." *Psychological Review* 129(4): 790–811.

Pink, D. 2022. *The Power of Regret: How Looking Backward Moves Us Forward*. New York: Riverhead Books.

Porges, S. 2022. "How to Use Polyvagal Theory to Re-Tune Your Nervous System and Feel Safe Enough to Be Yourself with Dr. Stephen Porges." Your Life in Process (podcast), hosted by D. Hill. https://drdianahill.com/051-how-to-use-polyvagal-theory-to -re-tune-your-nervous-system-and-feel-safe-enough-to-be-yourself-with-dr-stephen-porges.

Powers, T. A., and D. C. Zuroff. 1988. "Interpersonal Consequences of Overt Self-Criticism: A Comparison with Neutral and Self-Enhancing Presentations of Self." *Journal of Personality and Social Psychology* 54(6): 1054–62.

Price, C. J., and C. Hooven. 2018. "Interoceptive Awareness Skills for Emotion Regulation: Theory and Approach of Mindful Awareness in Body-Oriented Therapy (MABT)." *Frontiers in Psychology* 9: 798.

Siegel, D. J. 2022. *IntraConnected: MWe (Me + We) as the Integration of Self, Identity, and Belonging*. New York: W. W. Norton & Company.

Smith, J. L., and F. B. Bryant. 2017. "Savoring and Well-Being: Mapping the Cognitive-Emotional Terrain of the Happy Mind." In *The Happy Mind: Cognitive Contributions to Well-Being*, edited by M. D. Robinson and M. Eid, 139–56. New York: Springer International Publishing/Springer Nature.

Smith, W. K., and M. W. Lewis. 2022. *Both/And Thinking: Embracing Creative Tensions to Solve Your Toughest Problems*. Boston: Harvard Business Review Press.

Tawwab, N. 2022. "How to Set Boundaries and Find Peace with Nedra Tawwab." Your Life in Process (podcast), hosted by D. Hill. https://drdianahill.com/014-how-to-set -boundaries-and-find-peace-with-nedra-tawwab.

Tirch, D., B. Schoendorff, and L. R. Silberstein. 2014. *The ACT Practitioner's Guide to the Science of Compassion: Tools for Fostering Psychological Flexibility*. Oakland, CA: New Harbinger Publications.

Ward, L. 2020. *America's Racial Karma: An Invitation to Heal*. Berkeley, CA: Parallax Press.

———. 2022. "America's Racial Karma and a Tribute to Thich Nhat Hanh with Larry Ward." Your Life in Process (podcast), hosted by D. Hill. https://drdianahill.com/008 -americas-racial-karma-and-a-tribute-to-thich-nhat-hanh-with-dr-larry-ward.

Weis, R., and E. C. Speridakos. 2011. "A Meta-Analysis of Hope Enhancement Strategies in Clinical and Community Settings." *Psychology of Well-Being: Theory, Research and Practice* 1, 5. https://doi.org/10.1186/2211-1522-1-5.

Weller, F. 2015. *The Wild Edge of Sorrow: Rituals of Renewal and the Sacred Work of Grief*. Berkeley, CA: North Atlantic Books.

Younger, J., A. Aron, S. Parke, N. Chatterjee, and S. Mackey. 2010. "Viewing Pictures of a Romantic Partner Reduces Experimental Pain: Involvement of Neural Reward Systems." *PLOS ONE* 5(10): e13309. https://doi.org/10.1371/journal.pone.0013309.

Diana Hill, PhD, is a clinical psychologist, international trainer, and sought-after speaker on acceptance and commitment therapy (ACT) and compassion. Host of the podcast, *Your Life in Process*—and coauthor, with Debbie Sorenson, of *ACT Daily Journal*—Diana works with organizations, high-achievers, and health professionals who are committed to becoming psychologically flexible so they can transform their mental health at work, home, and around the globe. Diana practices what she preaches in her daily life as a mom of two boys, bee guardian, and yoga practitioner in Santa Barbara, CA.

Foreword writer **Joseph V. Ciarrochi, PhD,** is a professor at the Institute for Positive Psychology and Education at Australian Catholic University. He has published more than 160 scientific journal articles and many books, including the widely acclaimed *Emotional Intelligence in Everyday Life* and *The Weight Escape*.

MORE BOOKS from
NEW HARBINGER PUBLICATIONS

Did you know there are **free tools** you can download for this book?

Free tools are things like **worksheets, guided meditation exercises**, and **more** that will help you get the most out of your book.

You can download free tools for this book— whether you bought or borrowed it, in any format, from any source—from the New Harbinger website. All you need is a NewHarbinger.com account. Just use the URL provided in this book to view the free tools that are available for it. Then, click on the "download" button for the free tool you want, and follow the prompts that appear to log in to your NewHarbinger.com account and download the material.

You can also save the free tools for this book to your **Free Tools Library** so you can access them again anytime, just by logging in to your account! Just look for this button on the book's free tools page.

+ Save this to my free tools library